PUB STROLLS IN
HERTFORDSHIRE

Alan Charles

COUNTRYSIDE BOOKS
NEWBURY BERKSHIRE

First published 2002
© Alan Charles 2002
Revised and updated 2006

COUNTRYSIDE BOOKS
3 Catherine Road
Newbury, Berkshire

To view our complete range of books,
please visit us at
www.countrysidebooks.co.uk

ISBN 1 85306 724 5
EAN 978 1 85306 724 2

Designed by Graham Whiteman
Photographs by the author

Produced through MRM Associates Ltd., Reading
Printed in Singapore

Contents

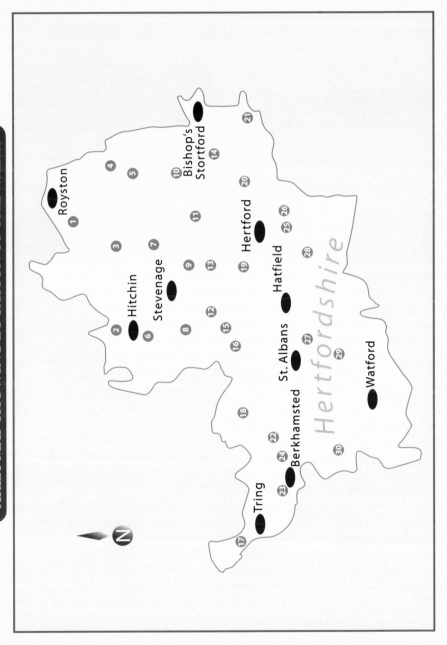

AREA MAP SHOWING LOCATION OF THE WALKS

PUBLISHER'S NOTE

We hope that you obtain considerable enjoyment from this book. Although at the time of publication all routes followed public rights of way or permitted paths, diversion orders can be made and permissions withdrawn.

We cannot, of course, be held responsible for such diversion orders and any inaccuracies in the text which result from these or any other changes to the routes nor any damage which might result from walkers trespassing on private property. We are anxious though that all details covering the walks are kept up to date and would therefore welcome information from readers which would be relevent to future editions.

The simple sketch maps that accompany the walk in this book are based on notes made by the author whilst checking out the routes on the ground. They are designed to show you how to reach the start and to point out the main features of the overall circuit.

However, for the benefit of a proper map, we do recommend that you purchase the relevant Ordnance Survey sheet covering your walk. Ordnance Survey maps are widely available, especially through booksellers and local newsagents.

Hertfordshire's great popularity with walkers is as much to do with its variety of landscape as with its marvellous network of footpaths and bridleways. The contrast between town and country is another factor, in that the busy urban life can be easily exchanged for the tranquillity and restorative powers of the countryside. It is in this countryside that we have a heritage of delightful village pubs, where the attractions of tradition go hand in hand with modern-day expectations – comfort, cleanliness, variety and quality in food and drink. The pubs featured here have been chosen because they conform to this ideal. Most can be described as 'real' village hostelries.

Many of the pubs retain what I have referred to as 'traditional' hours, with two opening sessions each day – usually 12 noon to 3 pm and 6 pm to 11 pm, give or take half an hour to an hour. This is often extended to 'all day' on Fridays and at weekends, where the traditional afternoon closure is laid aside. Some pubs choose to close completely on certain days – usually Mondays. Some do not provide food on Sundays, or if they do it may be confined to a 'roast only' lunch. And there are others which, although open for drinking, do not provide food on certain weekdays. Since walking on an empty stomach is not the ideal way to enjoy Hertfordshire, it is well worth reading the pub description before setting out!

Sunday is often a busy period at country pubs, especially at lunchtime, and to be guaranteed a meal at that time it is advisable to book a table in advance. Most of the pubs have their own car parks. If you wish to leave your car there while on the walk you should check with the landlord first (you should, of course, be a customer). Alternatively, if you opt for roadside parking please take care not to block any exits and entrances.

The routes for these thirty strolls are all circular – beginning and ending at the pub – and are easily undertaken, varying in length from $1^3/_4$ to $3^3/_4$ miles. Much of the walking is along well-used footpaths and bridleways.

The walks may be followed on the superb Explorer series of Ordnance Survey maps. These are on a scale of $2^1/_2$ inches to the mile and show public rights of way in considerable detail. Twenty-two of the walks are covered by sheets 182 and 194, the remainder by sheets 174, 181 and 193. The OS/Philips Street Atlas for Hertfordshire is a useful alternative. It is also on a scale of $2^1/_2$ inches to the mile and is available in a cheap paperback edition. In addition to showing footpaths and bridleways (but not their status as rights of way) it gives the names of streets, farms, larger houses and pubs.

Given good weather (and good health of course!) you should find these walks easy-going, stimulating and enjoyable. And at the pubs you should find relaxation and a welcoming atmosphere. So here's wishing you thirty memorable days of discovery – and many further opportunities to rewalk your favourite routes – in this lovely county of Hertfordshire!

Alan Charles

Therfield
The Fox & Duck

MAP: OS EXPLORER 194 (GR 336373)	**WALK 1**	DISTANCE: 2¼ MILES

DIRECTIONS TO START: THERFIELD IS SIGNPOSTED FROM THE A10 2½ MILES SOUTH OF ROYSTON AND FROM THE A505 BETWEEN ROYSTON AND BALDOCK. FOR THE SHORTEST DRIVE FROM THE A10 LOOK FOR A TALL RADIO MAST AND A ROADSIDE CAFÉ AND LEAVE THE A10 AT THAT POINT! THE FOX & DUCK IS EASILY FOUND BY THE GREEN AT THERFIELD. **PARKING:** IN THE PUB'S CAR PARK OR ALONGSIDE THE GREEN NEARBY.

Therfield – an outpost of Hertfordshire but contributing in no small measure to the county's character and attractiveness. This and the superb views to be enjoyed across the neighbouring county of Cambridgeshire make this a very special place, particularly for walkers.

On leaving the village green the walk makes straight for the escarpment where the skylarks are calling and where the views must be seen to be believed. Turning 'inland' it meets the road at Washingtonditch Green and returns to Therfield by way of Hay Green Farm and a crossing of the Icknield Way Path.

The Fox & Duck

An unassuming pub in its outward appearance but a revelation when you enter! The bar area opens out to a large dining room where customers clearly take delight in the ambience and in their chosen meal. And with no less than eight blackboard menus arranged around the walls, that choice requires some premeditation. The 'Bar meals' list includes well-known dishes such as steak and kidney pudding, chicken tikka and chilli con carne. 'Starters and snacks' offers such delicacies as grilled goat's cheese and deep fried lobster tails, while the 'Gourmet menu' concentrates on more exotic dishes. Ricotta, spinach and goat's cheese cannelloni is one of a selection of interesting vegetarian dishes, while 'Chef's specials' and 'Fish specials' enlarge the choice still further. There is also a children's menu and a sweets menu. A good range of Courage ales is offered; also an amazing choice of wines from all corners of the world.

The pub is open every day at the traditional hours, with some flexibility at weekends. Meals are served every lunchtime and evening except Sunday evening. In addition to a roast, a full menu is offered at Sunday lunchtime, when it is well worth booking a table in advance. Dogs are not permitted inside the pub. Telephone: 01763 287246.

The Walk

① The walk commences at a rough drive labelled 'Icknield Way' alongside the pub. This soon runs into private property where a waymark post beckons you forward into a short path on the left. On entering the

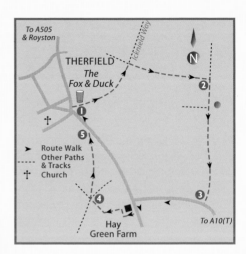

fields cross these straight on to the far left-hand corner; then go half-left in the next field, aiming for a gap at the mid-point of the low scrub on the far side. On arrival turn right at a crossing into a signposted path running between hedges – then shortly experience an amazing view across Cambridgeshire! Stay with the level path for ⅓ mile between fields, while following a sparse hedge on the right.

② When the hedge terminates and a large field blocks the way ahead, turn right into a farm track and aim for the right-hand edge of a copse some distance ahead, where a 'private' track comes in from the right. Keep forward to a hedge corner – which will be on your right – and follow the hedge and its accompanying ditch straight on and into the next field. Ignore a wide gap in the trees and drop down to a sunken path on the right. This is about 150 yards prior to the field's far corner and soon bears off to the right through the scrub. It passes to the right of a pond and emerges at a road.

③ Turn right in the road and follow this through to a T-junction, passing Meadow

Therfield

Way and a housing estate as you go. Turn left at the T-junction into Rooks Nest Lane and leave it for a path on the right after about 50 yards. Go through the hedge gap here and turn right immediately, hugging the field edge all the way around Hay Green Farm. After navigating around at least six corners and remaining close to the field edge, you will eventually meet a footbridge on the right – which you could easily miss, and which is 20 yards beyond a corner.

④ Go over the footbridge and immediately find yourself on a track – the Icknield Way again. Cross the track to a gate opposite and from there go half-right to another gate in the furthest corner of the field. Cross the next field in the same direction to another gate – where there's a thatched cottage in view to the right – and

there enter a much larger field. This final field is subdivided by a line of trees for part of its length, and you should walk with these trees to your right. If in doubt note the destination of the furthest run of overhead wires and make your way to the same point.

⑤ Leave the field through a gate in its corner and walk along a short path to the road (Police Row!). Turn left in the road for the village green and the Fox & Duck.

> ### PLACES OF INTEREST NEARBY
> **Therfield Heath** is 1½ miles north of Therfield village, in the Royston direction. Described as 'the largest area of flower-rich chalk grassland remaining in Hertfordshire', it is particularly prized for its colony of pasque flowers. It is also a much-favoured area for birds and butterflies.

Ickleford
The Plume of Feathers

DIRECTIONS TO START: ICKLEFORD IS A SHORT DISTANCE FROM THE NORTHERN EXTREMITY OF HITCHIN. IF DRIVING NORTH FROM HITCHIN ALONG THE A600 IN THE BEDFORD DIRECTION, TURN RIGHT INTO TURNPIKE LANE SHORTLY AFTER CROSSING THE RIVER OUGHTON. THE PLUME OF FEATHERS WILL BE FOUND BEHIND UPPER GREEN NEAR ICKLEFORD'S PARISH CHURCH. **PARKING:** IN THE PUB'S CAR PARK OR ALONG THE ROADSIDE IN UPPER GREEN.

This is Icknield Way country, where the ancient route links the vastness of Letchworth to the smallness of Ickleford. With its Norman church, its Upper Green and its attractive flint-built village school, Ickleford is a world apart from its southern neighbour, Hitchin.

In following the line of the Icknield Way, the walk crosses the river Oughton and the route of the former Hitchin to Bedford railway. Magnificent vistas abound as the walk climbs gently but continuously to Wilbury Hill, and an almost mirror image reversal along fieldside paths returns it to lower ground. A pleasant conclusion to the walk is enjoyed as the route crosses level pastures from Cadwell Farm back to Ickleford's Upper Green.

The Plume of Feathers

The Plume of Feathers can look back across the centuries to a tradition of service to the village. In the 1700s a blacksmith's shop was attached to what was then a private house. In the 1800s a wheelwright's craft went side-by-side with victualling. Today this busy pub is fully absorbed in providing good food and drink, for which it is justly famous.

Divided into a public bar and lounge, the pub clearly meets the needs of those calling in for a drink and a chat as well as those who come for a meal in restaurant-style comfort. One of the secrets of the pub's popularity today lies in its food. With such a wide-ranging menu, the only difficulty is in making a choice! Along with starters, there are meat dishes (steaks, mushroom stroganoff, chicken Creole, for example), pasta dishes, omelettes, fish dishes, homemade pies, salads, ploughman's, filled jacket potatoes, sandwiches and baguettes. There is also a choice of very tempting desserts. The complete menu is available at lunchtimes and in the evenings every day, except Sunday evenings. This is supplemented by a roast lunch on Sundays, for which prior booking is essential. Traditional opening hours are kept Monday to Thursday, with 'all day' opening from Friday to Sunday; so there are plenty of opportunities to enjoy one of the pub's six real ales! Telephone: 01462 432729.

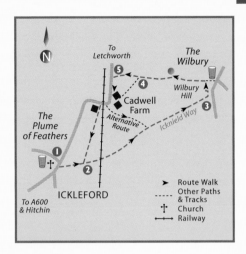

Upper Green, Ickleford

The Walk

① From the Plume of Feathers go along Upper Green to the main road and cross this to the rough drive opposite. This is to the right of a public shelter and signposted 'Icknield Way'. Passing between houses the drive soon terminates at a gate, which gives access to an attractive green space. Keep forward here – along the left-hand border –

and soon cross the river Oughton to another green space. The brick abutment on the left is a remnant of the former Hitchin to Bedford railway which crossed the Icknield Way at this point. Surprising as it may seem, this was once part of the main line of the Midland Railway to London. It became a cross-country route and finally closed in 1962. Opposite the abutment an information board relates the misfortune of Gerry, who drowned in the nearby lake after a late night at the pub. So be warned! Now known as Gerry's Pond the lake has become a haven for wildlife.

② Continuing forward from the pond soon cross the modern railway footbridge and walk alongside a substantial metal fence. A magnificent panorama opens up and, later, a path comes in from the left; and a nearby seat is a welcome accompaniment to the walk. Keeping straight as before, you will, after a further ½ mile, meet the road at Wilbury Hill.

③ Go through a gate on the left just before the road and follow a path through the shrubbery to a gap on the left. From this point you could go forward to a small picnic area situated under a stand of Scots pine trees; but to continue on the walk you should turn left through the gap. After passing the second of two seats and having ignored a branch on the right, you will arrive at a T-junction in the path. This is just beyond a footbridge. Here you have another choice: turn right for the Wilbury, a popular roadside pub, or left through a gate to continue on the walk. Assuming the latter, you will be accompanied by a hedge on the right, and, after ¼ mile, the border of a long narrow wood, Fox Covert.

④ When the path becomes a track and turns half-left towards Cadwell Farm, don't be so engrossed with other thoughts that you turn left with it, but leave it at this point and go forward along a field edge. The path passes through the right-hand hedge after 200 yards and continues downhill as before, to meet a road.

⑤ Turn left at the road and follow it down to the railway bridge by Cadwell Farm; then take great care as you walk under the bridge to the far side. If you prefer to avoid the bridge you could turn left *before* it and join a path running between gardens and opposite a pond. Continuing forward across fields and along a farm track you will eventually return to the Icknield Way, where a right turn repeats – in reverse – the first part of the walk. Otherwise, leave the road immediately beyond the bridge by joining a short drive on the left. The drive runs alongside the house numbered '1' (there is only one!) and terminates at a gate and stile. Your route is now more or less straight on by way of one very long field followed by a small field. In the process you will gradually move away from the railway and, after ½ mile (measured from the bridge), arrive back at the Icknield Way. The final connection with the Way is made at a stile in its bordering hedge. Turn right there and retrace your steps back to Upper Green and the Plume of Feathers.

PLACES OF INTEREST NEARBY
The **Hitchin Museum and Art Gallery** at Paynes Park in nearby Hitchin contains many fascinating exhibits, including an old chemist's shop and a medicinal plant garden. It is open 10 am to 5 pm daily, except Wednesday and Sunday. Telephone: 01462 434476.

Rushden
The Moon & Stars

DIRECTIONS TO START: RUSHDEN IS SIGNPOSTED FROM THE A507
(WHERE IT DESCRIBES A 'DOG LEG') MIDWAY BETWEEN BALDOCK AND BUNTINGFORD.
DRIVE NORTH FROM THE A507 FOR ONE MILE, BUT DON'T TURN RIGHT INTO THE
'NO THROUGH ROAD' SIGNPOSTED TO RUSHDEN. INSTEAD CONTINUE FORWARD
FOR THE SHORT DISTANCE TO THE PUB. **PARKING:** AT THE FRONT OF THE PUB OR ALONG
THE ROADSIDE NEARBY.

Descending the road down into Rushden from the A507, the splendid view ahead is but a token of what is to come. The village, together with its outlier Southern Green, is pure delight. The lovely thatched cottages are so numerous and so beautifully placed that you could well imagine yourself in an open-air folk museum!

Tracing a figure-of-eight around Rushden and Southern Green, the walk reveals all this delight. It visits the church and explores mostly well-kept footpaths near Batchelor's Wood, and in the process enjoys fine views of Julians, an impressive 18th century manor house.

The Moon & Stars

Such is the Moon & Stars' reputation that visitors from far and near join local residents here to enjoy good ale, good food and good wine.

The lunch menu is ideal for walkers whether their preference is for a light lunch – soup, sandwiches or ploughmans for example – or something more substantial – such as steak, Guinness and stilton pie, smoked gammon ham, or whole tail scampi – and all prepared by the landlord's own hand, whose previous experience at the Bull, Cottered, helped to win that pub its inclusion in the Michelin Guide.

An alternative menu is available each evening with the exception of Sunday and Monday. It includes an extensive choice of starters, main courses and desserts. In winter you can enjoy all this in the warmth of real open fires, or, in summer, in the large garden at the rear. Ales available include Greene King IPA and Shepherd and Neame Spitfire.

The pub keeps traditional hours from Monday to Saturday. It is open 'all day' on Sundays during the summer months and closes at 6 pm on Sundays in winter. The landlord goes out of his way to welcome walking parties, large or small – especially when meals are ordered in advance! Telephone: 01763 288330.

The Walk

① Cross the road from the Moon & Stars to a footbridge over the diminutive river Beane. Passing a house at the start soon go over a stile and head straight on uphill between tall trees to the churchyard at the

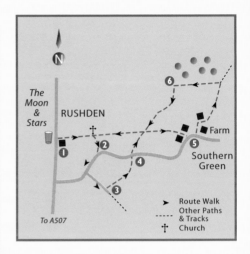

top. You may well find the church open. Since this is unusual these days, you could take advantage of the fact! My first impressions were of a pleasant uncluttered church with a fine timbered roof and pews.

② Turning right from the church, leave the churchyard along the drive and soon join a road, Church End, at a bend. Turn right into Church End and follow this between all the picturesque cottages to the first turning on the left, Treacle Lane, a street name demanding explanation! In its earlier unmade state the surface could be reminiscent of treacle. It also had a sweet shop – and the present Treacle Cottage was that shop!

③ Fifty yards before Treacle Lane's tarmac gives way to gravel turn left into a wide grassy path bordering a bungalow – which looks a little out of place in Rushden! This point is opposite the garden of Flint Cottage. Soon enter a field at its corner and walk the left-hand edge of this and the next field, alongside a fence in the second field and following overhead wires all the way.

④ At the road ahead cross to a path under trees opposite and follow this through to a meeting of paths. With all the timber decking laid so meticulously at the crossing it is clear that the County Council rights of way team have taken great pains to keep our feet dry! Turn right at the crossing and soon enter a field at its corner. You will now need to cross this field to a point halfway along its opposite border – to the right of the thatched house seen face-on. On arrival pass between gardens and soon join the road at Southern Green.

⑤ Turn left in the road and leave it when it very soon curves to the right, and there join the drive to Southern Green Farm. After passing a pond follow the concrete drive round to the right – between a huge barn and 'Haybarn', a farmhouse. Turn left beyond the farmhouse and cross a field downhill towards the right-hand border of a wood (Batchelor's Wood) at the bottom. If you make a close pass of an electricity pole on an island of grass on the way down, you are on the correct course. On meeting another electricity pole with wires branching three ways, keep forward a few yards and turn left; then walk beside the wood edge, with a ditch running parallel to your left, all the way to the end of the trees.

⑥ Ignore the track going forward from the wood end to a field and turn left into a path under a narrow band of trees. You will have a good view of the manor house, Julians, distantly across the fields. Stay with the path all the way to the timber-decked crossing that we met earlier and turn right there through a kissing-gate (this crossing

Church End, Rushden

should not be confused with an earlier T-junction in the path where timber decking is also used). Walk the right-hand edge of the next two fields and enter the churchyard once more; then pass to the left of the church and continue forward through the gate opposite. Descend the slope ahead to a stile by the right-hand of two houses and soon cross the footbridge opposite the Moon & Stars.

PLACES OF INTEREST NEARBY
Cromer's restored windmill is two miles south of Rushden. It is open from 2.30 pm to 5 pm on Sundays and bank holidays and on the second and fourth Saturdays in each month from mid-May to mid-September. From Rushden you could drive south to the windmill along a route that includes a short stretch of the A507. Telephone: 01279 843301.

Anstey
The Chequers

DIRECTIONS TO START: ANSTEY IS SIGNPOSTED FROM THE B1368 ONE MILE WEST OF THE VILLAGE. THE B1368 IS A PLEASANT DRIVE NORTH FROM THE A10 AT PUCKERIDGE.
PARKING: IN THE PUB'S CAR PARK OR ALONG THE ROADSIDE NEARBY.

Women gossiping at the village well; children watching the shoemaker and the blacksmith at work; the butcher, the general store, the post office, the dairy. All have gone, but the beauty remains, the beauty that overflows into the surrounding countryside – along its well-kept footpaths, in its fields and meadows and in its snatches of woodland.

The walk draws on all of this as it works its way south to Daw's End, returning through Snow End and through St George's churchyard and under the shadow of the massive castle-less motte and bailey.

The Chequers

When speaking to landlords I occasionally ask if their pub is *not* haunted, since that would be unusual! It seems that the Chequers *is* haunted, but not by the US airmen who came here during the Second World War from Nuthampstead airfield. Doubtless they came mainly for the ale. Local residents and visitors come here today for the food as well.

Of most interest to walkers is the lunchtime bar menu, which is more than adequate for most appetites. It includes sandwiches, burgers, filled jacket potatoes, ploughman's, ham, sausages, chicken and scampi. If you came out in a rush and missed your breakfast, you could try the pub's 'all day' version. The restaurant menu is for evening dining only and offers a wide choice of main courses and desserts. Also included is an interesting selection of vegetarian dishes – Mediterranean bean ragout and tomato and basil penne, for example. Booking is essential for the Sunday lunch, which, in addition to a roast, includes a choice of starters, speciality steaks and sweets. The bar menu is not in use at that time. The Chequers is a free house and usually offers three real ales and a selection of 18 wines, including champagne. Children are welcome and have their own special menu. Surprisingly for a small village, the pub is open 'all day, every day', with meals served every lunchtime and evening except Sunday evening. Telephone: 01763 848205.

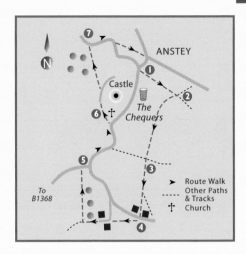

The Walk

① Turn right on leaving the Chequers and walk as far as the village well at the road junction. Go over the stile on the right here and follow the path alongside gardens and a field edge and gradually downhill to the field corner.

② After crossing a footbridge in the corner turn very sharp right around a scrubby hedge and follow a field edge. You should have a good view of Anstey church as you make your way along the field edge to a gap at the far end. Keep forward across the next two fields, crossing another footbridge as you go and meeting a hedge corner a little uphill on the far side.

③ Walking straight on and gradually uphill, and keeping company with a hedge and ditch, eventually meet a footbridge on the right where the hedge terminates. Cross the footbridge and enter the paddock through a gate. Go uphill across the grass, leaving the paddock through another gate and passing midway between two houses before joining a road.

The old well at Anstey

of the church. Do break off at this point and go inside the church. A brief guide is available which includes a note on the stained glass window in the south aisle to the left of the porch (as viewed from the inside). This is in memory of the US airmen based at nearby Nuthampstead airfield who died during the Second World War. The window was dedicated and unveiled on 11th June 2000.

⑥ Passing to the left of the church, leave the churchyard and go forward along a drive – but for a short distance only – with the huge motte and bailey and its moat on your right. This is all that remains of a Norman castle. Now don't stay in the drive but leave it before it turns right and go forward into a paddock by way of a curious stile, aiming for the right-hand edge of the wood on the far side. Climb an identical stile and cross a ditch by the wood corner and follow the wood edge out to the road by thatched Woodside Cottage.

④ Cross the road to a short track opposite. Turn right off the track very soon (a few yards only) at the first hedge corner and enter a path between hedges on the right. The path eventually evolves into a drive leading to two cottages, the second being Welspen Thatch. Keep straight on from the latter, between a hedge and a wood and out into a field. Go forward a few yards and turn right around the wood corner. At an indent in the field edge leave the field for a path by going straight on, soon passing between gardens and meeting a road by the house 'Snowden'.

⑤ Turn right in the road and left at the T-junction. Anstey church comes into view as you make your way along the road, downhill at first then uphill to the lychgate

⑦ Turn right and leave the road just after it bends right and cross the left-hand field half right to its far right-hand corner, then turn right at the road for the Chequers. Alternatively, you could stay on the road all the way back to the well at Anstey (less than ¼ mile), turning right again for the Chequers.

PLACES OF INTEREST NEARBY

The site of **Nuthampstead's wartime airfield** is one mile north-east of Anstey. In the Second World War it was a base of the 398th Bomb Group, US Air Force. A memorial to the Group can be seen outside the Woodman public house in Nuthampstead village. From Anstey you will need to rejoin the B1368 and drive north to Barkway, turning right there for Nuthampstead.

Great Hormead
The Three Tuns

MAP: OS EXPLORER 194 (GR 402300) | **WALK 5** | **DISTANCE:** 2¼ MILES

DIRECTIONS TO START: GREAT HORMEAD IS EASILY APPROACHED FROM BUNTINGFORD ALONG THE B1038 VIA HARE STREET. ON ARRIVAL AT HARE STREET TURN LEFT INTO THE B1368, THEN BACK INTO THE B1038 BY TURNING RIGHT ALMOST IMMEDIATELY (ROAD SIGNS UNCLEAR HERE). BUNTINGFORD ITSELF IS CONNECTED TO THE A10 AT TWO PLACES. **PARKING:** THE PUB HAS ITS OWN CAR PARK. ALTERNATIVELY, DRIVE TO THE CHURCH AND LEAVE YOUR CAR AT THE ROADSIDE, STARTING THE WALK AT POINT 2.

'Great' and 'Little' are appropriate prefixes for two delightful Hormead settlements; and judging from the presence of some huge barns in the area and the fact that Great Hormead had two windmills, these settlements were central to a thriving agricultural community. Today many residents travel elsewhere to their place of work, while living in the cottages that reflect an earlier age.

The walk alternates between quiet country roads and easily navigated footpaths. Among its highlights are the lovely cottages at both Great and Little Hormead, the attractive settings of each of the two churches, and the views across the valley where lies Hare Street and the river Quin.

The Three Tuns

The Three Tuns owes its present appearance to a disastrous fire that occurred in 1991. It took two years to rise from the ashes and is now a very popular 'food destination' pub, attractive inside and out. The bar has kept its original fireplace – with its interesting fireback – while the light and airy restaurant is set with cottage-style furniture.

The food menu is available lunchtimes and evenings (Sundays 12.30 pm to 3 pm) and offers a wide spectrum of main meals and daily specials. This varies according to the season. Being only a few miles from the lovely village of Braughing, it is not surprising that the famous Braughing sausages are on the menu. Sirloin and rib-eye steaks are also included, as are home-made fish cakes and beer-battered fresh fish. For those with a reduced appetite a choice of 'lite bites' and sandwiches is available. Children are catered for with half portions of 'adult' meals.

There are three real ales – Greene King IPA, Abbot Ale and a 'rotating' guest bitter. While the pub keeps traditional opening hours Monday to Saturday, it is open 'all day' on Sundays. Telephone: 01763 289409.

The Walk

① From the road junction by the Three Tuns go uphill along Horseshoe Hill and follow the twists and turns of the road (pass to the right of the war memorial) until you are within 150 yards of St Nicholas' church – by a speed derestriction sign. Go over a stile on the right here and walk the very short path to a field corner. Turn left and

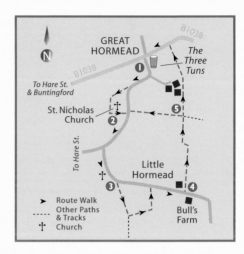

follow the upper field edge (while enjoying the superb view!) for 150 yards to a stile and gate on the left, by a cattle trough. The stile places you on another short path, this one leading to a churchyard gate. Passing to the right of the church soon rejoin the road on the far side. I know there is a quicker way to this point, but that would mean missing the view!

② Turn right at the road (go forward if parked by the church) and follow this all the way to a junction. Turn left there for Little Hormead and go past St Mary's church (which is celebrated for its 800 year old door) to a signposted gap on the right by a dip in the road. This is about 120 yards beyond the church and gives access to the second field corner.

③ Go along the left-hand field edge, followed by only a short length (35 yards) of the next field edge. This point coincides with the shallow summit of the field. Go left into a path here and stay with it when it turns left. On arrival at the road ahead, turn right and walk through the village, passing an attractive

An old barn has been converted to a desirable residence at Little Hormead

cottage terrace and a massive barn, which has been converted to private dwellings.

④ Leave the road just beyond the 'barn' and join a footpath on the left opposite Bull's Farm. Then follow a left-hand field edge, with a garden in view all the way. Keep forward into the next field, but now along its right-hand edge and with a hedge on the right. This leads to yet another field, in which you should go briefly left before continuing forward. On meeting a rough drive at the far end of this – the third – field you have the option of walking directly back to Great

Hormead church, where you may have left your car. For this simply turn left through a hedge gap and cross the field to the church.

⑤ To return to the village and the Three Tuns go straight on along the track and, when it turns left en-route to a housing estate (which may be hidden from your view) keep forward across a field to a stile, following a hedge for part of the way and in the general direction of overhead power lines. Descend the next field to another stile, while following overhead wires; then pass between gardens to a road. Turn left for the Three Tuns.

Charlton
The Windmill

DIRECTIONS TO START: CHARLTON IS SIGNPOSTED FROM THE A602 SOUTH-WEST OF HITCHIN. LEAVE THE A602 WHERE IT CROSSES THE RIVER HIZ AND SOON TURN LEFT FOR CHARLTON. THE A602 CONNECTS WITH JUNCTION 8 OF THE A1(M). TAKE CARE NOT TO TAKE THE A602 FROM JUNCTION 7! **PARKING:** IN THE PUB'S CAR PARK. ROADSIDE PARKING IS POSSIBLE BUT NOT IDEAL – UNLESS YOU TOUCH DOWN A FEW HUNDRED YARDS PRIOR TO THE PUB!

If this is to be your first visit to Charlton, you will be surprised to find such a delightfully rural retreat so close to the town of Hitchin. The river Hiz rises in the fields here and a quiet country lane heads away from the settlement and up to the undulating slopes of the Chiltern escarpment at its most northerly extremity.

The walk samples a little of the escarpment, which forms a superb panorama throughout much of the excursion. It connects with a short stretch of the country lane, and skirts the fields where the river Hiz commences its youthful journey from an attractively sited pond.

The Windmill

Charlton's windmill is preserved in name only – in that of the pub and in Windmill Lane nearby. Having come to grief in the late 1800s, only the base of the mill remains. Its namesake, the Windmill pub, thrives to the present day, as is evidenced in its comfort and welcome, in its food and its ale.

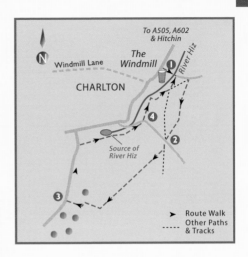

Food is available from 12 noon to 2.30 pm and 6 pm to 9 pm on Monday to Friday, 12 noon to 9 pm on Saturday and 12 noon to 8 pm on Sunday. The regular menu caters for a wide spectrum of appetites, from the keen to the light. Steaks come in sirloin, rump and gammon. Main meals include game pie, chicken balti, and 'traditional fish and chips', while the 'light selection' includes filled jacket potatoes, sandwiches and baguettes. Examples from the specials boards are bacon and onion suet pudding and Viking gammon – gammon topped with melted cheese and tomato. A choice of vegetarian dishes is offered; also a selection of traditional puddings.

Opening hours are 11 am to 3 pm and 6 pm to 11 pm on Monday and 'all day' Tuesday to Sunday; so there are plenty of opportunities to sample one of the Charles Wells real ales or the guest ale. For those who prefer wine, there is a good range. In winter you will enjoy the warmth and crackle of the wood-burning stove, in summer the murmur of the river Hiz as it flows past the pub's patio garden. Telephone: 01462 432096.

The Walk

① Cross the river Hiz by turning right out of the Windmill and go uphill on what seems a cross between a tarmac footpath and a narrow lane. After passing thatched Ivy Cottage, ignore the first footpath on the right and continue to the top of the hill. Go through a gap on the right there and enter a field at its corner. Ignoring a branching path crossing the field diagonally, go along the field edge, with a hedge on your left – and enjoy some fabulous views!

② On arrival at a lane, cross to the track opposite and go along this for 60 yards to the bridleway (it may look like a footpath!) on the right. Go through the hedge gap here and follow the left-hand hedge along what is a very large field – and enjoy yet more fabulous views! Continue forward in the next field (there is no separating hedge), into a dip and then under high voltage electricity wires, and soon bear right towards a wood. The path has now become a track and as such curves to the left just prior to the wood. It passes briefly under trees and descends the hill to a road.

③ Turn right and go along this

The source of the river Hiz at Charlton

delightfully peaceful road for ¼ mile or so to a footpath on the right. This point of departure is where the road dips noticeably 100 yards prior to its right-hand turn. The path will take you between fields and eventually in sight of a pond in a very attractive setting. This is the source of the river Hiz, a river that enhances not only Charlton but also the town of Hitchin through which it flows. By continuing along the field edge you will pass the boundary fence of Wellhead Farm, after which a lane runs parallel on the left.

④ You should join the lane from the far left-hand corner of the field (the lane turns right there) and cross to a metal kissing-gate opposite. A concrete drive runs forward from this point to a water pumping station, but the path parts company with the drive by veering slightly left across the grass. With the pumping station now over to the right, go forward to a stile, but without crossing it. Instead, turn right and walk uphill, with the pumping station's perimeter fence now on your right, and turn left when adjacent to the upper corner of the fence. Back on your previous orientation and along a left-hand field edge, ignore a right-hand branch at the summit of the field and continue following the field edge, with thatched Ivy Cottage in view down to your left. Stay with the field edge as far as the left hand corner and descend a short flight of steps to a lane. A left turn here will see you back at the Windmill in no time at all!

A wall plaque on Charlton House opposite the Windmill commemorates the 'inventor and engineer' Sir Henry Bessemer. He was born there in 1813 and is best known for inventing a method of manufacturing steel through the use of what became known as the Bessemer Converter.

Ardeley
The Jolly Waggoner

MAP: OS EXPLORER 194 WITH A SHORT STRETCH ON 193 (GR 310272)

WALK 7

DISTANCE: 3 MILES

DIRECTIONS TO START: ARDELEY IS SIGNPOSTED FROM THE B1037 AT THE SOUTHERN END OF CROMER. THE B1037 CAN BE ACCESSED FROM STEVENAGE OR FROM THE A507 AT COTTERED. **PARKING:** IN THE PUB'S CAR PARK OR IN SCHOOL LANE BY THE CHURCH. THERE ARE ALSO A FEW PARKING SPACES OPPOSITE THE VILLAGE HALL, WHICH IS NEAR THE CHURCH.

While the primary attraction that draws visitors to Ardeley seems to be the thatched houses around the village green, it may not be immediately obvious to them that the houses were built over a period as recent as 1917 to 1920! Genuinely old is the 13th century church, the 17th century Old Vicarage and, of course, the Jolly Waggoners – not forgetting Ardeley Bury, the manor house just outside the village.

The walk explores the bridleways and footpaths to the south of the village and those close to Ardeley Bury. It enjoys extensive views from these elevated ways – south towards Clay End, west to Walkern, and north towards Cromer. Since one of the bridleways is liable to be muddy, it is worth being well shod for this walk!

The Jolly Waggoner

No visitor to the Jolly Waggoner could argue with the *Good Pub Guide*'s commentary on this pub: '. . . a relaxed and civilised atmosphere'. And where food is concerned no one could classify it as anything other than first class. So much so that many of its customers show their appreciation by returning time and time again.

On the matter of choice, nothing is left to chance, with all degrees of appetite catered for. On the lunchtime menu there are sandwiches, ploughman's, salads, 'starters and light lunches', and a full English breakfast. Examples under the 'main courses' heading are fillet of chicken, locally made sausages, vegetable and pasta bake and omelette Arnold Bennett – an omelette filled with smoked haddock and served with béchamel sauce. And there are further choices on the specials boards – including desserts that will set your taste buds in a twirl!

In winter enjoy all this in the glow of the real log fire; in summer in the garden at the back or on the patio at the front – where you can watch the quiet world go by. Greene King real ales are dispensed from barrels behind the bar; and a good selection of wines is offered.

The pub keeps traditional hours every day, including weekends; and meals are served every lunchtime and evening, including Sunday evening. Telephone: 01438 861350.

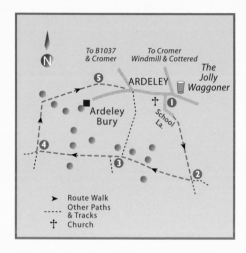

The Walk

① From the front door of the Jolly Waggoner go along the road and turn left into School Lane just prior to the church. The lane turns left and becomes a 'public byway' beyond the houses. Stay with the byway (just a track to you and me!) ignoring any branches as it descends to a dip and rises again between the fields, with trees as company for much of the way.

② At a junction of ways after ½ mile (measured from the village) turn right into a bridleway and go along this level route under the trees. On meeting a wood continue forward; and on emerging stay with its long narrow extension. Then enjoy the superb view that this elevated route allows. At a gap in the trees ahead a signpost points to Ardeley – but that's for information only!

③ The narrow band of trees continues forward from the gap, but you should now leave it by turning half-left and continuing forward again after a few yards. Although a bridleway signpost points left and downhill

The charming village green at Ardeley

after a further 100 yards, you should ignore this and go straight on across the large field, aiming for a gap in the thin line of conifer trees at the far end. Continue forward again from the gap, on a slightly raised path and with Walkern church in view ahead, staying the course downhill to the field end.

④ Ignore a kissing-gate under trees beyond the field corner and turn right along what is (curiously, since this is a footpath) waymarked with a black arrow. Follow the field edge – with a line of trees on the left – into the far left-hand corner; and on arrival go briefly under the trees to the field beyond. As you walk the right-hand edge of this next field (a half-right turn) you will be accompanied by a hedge and a low fence dividing the field from the grounds of Ardeley Bury. The attractive outbuildings of the Bury will come into view as you continue forward along the next field edge. You will also see the lake and, in winter, the house itself through the trees. Described as a 'strange Gothic fantasy', the house was once the home of Sir Henry Chauncy, a celebrated 17th century historian and author. Another lake makes an appearance under trees on your immediate right after you descend the next (the third) field to its corner.

⑤ Keeping forward in the final field go uphill to the top right-hand corner and join the road there.

Go forward along the road and in due course find yourself back at the Jolly Waggoner.

Whitwell
The Maiden's Head

MAP: OS EXPLORER 193 (GR 184211)　　**WALK 8**　　**DISTANCE:** 3¼ MILES

DIRECTIONS TO START: WHITWELL IS ON THE B651, A GOOD ROAD WHICH RUNS NORTH FROM ST ALBANS VIA WHEATHAMPSTEAD AND KIMPTON. AN ALTERNATIVE APPROACH IS FROM HARPENDEN ALONG THE B652, CONNECTING WITH THE B651 AT KIMPTON. IN PLACES THE B652 IS VERY NARROW, WITH BLIND MEANDERINGS.
PARKING: IN FRONT OF THE PUB OR IN ITS CAR PARK ON THE OPPOSITE SIDE OF THE ROAD. ROADSIDE PARKING IS ALSO POSSIBLE.

Perhaps the countryside around Whitwell is best known for its association with Queen Elizabeth the Queen Mother, who was baptised at St Paul's Walden and spent part of her childhood at The Bury. Such concentration of interest is likely to distract us from the lovely countryside around nearby Stagenhoe, a Sue Ryder home.

The walk sets off from Whitwell near the Nine Wells watercress farm and climbs gently between fields to Stagenhoe, where the views must be seen to be believed! It returns to Whitwell through woodland and along field edges, finally crossing the river Mimram, one of the delights of Whitwell.

The Maiden's Head

McMullen's Cellarmanship Award; Best Pub in all East Anglia; Best Community Pub Award. These are some of the accolades showered on this otherwise unassuming pub in this equally unassuming village. Step inside and discover exactly what all this means. Firstly: the quality of its real ales – all from McMullen's local Hertfordshire brewery. Secondly: the welcome and the ambience – helped along in winter by two real log fires. Thirdly: the variety of food that is on offer. Whether you are a hearty or a light eater, you should go away satisfied and sustained. At the top of the bill there are rump and sirloin steaks. Then comes gammon with pineapple, ham off the joint, breaded plaice stuffed with prawns, scampi, seafood platter, chicken curry, chilli con carne and 'Pollo' – a dish of chicken pieces cooked in white wine sauce. Sandwiches come in three types – 'open', 'closed' and 'toasted'; and there is an extensive choice of salads and ploughman's.

The pub is open more or less at the traditional hours, with no all day opening; and meals are available at lunchtimes and in the evenings from Monday to Saturday, except Monday evening. Food on Sundays is limited to sandwiches and ploughman's at lunchtimes and in summer only. For something more than this on Sundays you will need go to the Bull just along the road.

Choose a dry day if your children are with you, for they can only be accommodated in the garden. Telephone: 01438 871392.

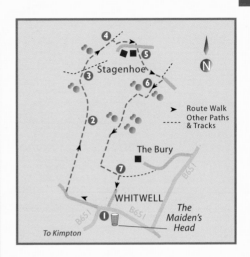

The Walk

① Go left along the road from the Maiden's Head and keep straight on past the garden centre to the watercress farm. After the road describes a minor S-bend at the far end of the watercress farm leave it for a track on the right signposted 'Preston 2½'. This track will take you gradually uphill, escorted by randomly placed trees.

② Keeping forward through a wide gap at the top of the hill you will soon start to descend. And as you follow the track downhill across a field you will get nearer to a wood on the left, while enjoying a magnificent view across Stagenhoe Park to your right.

③ On meeting a track running up from a dip, cross over from a waymark post and go uphill between fields, aiming for the right-hand end of a wood at the top. After walking just inside the wood, you will emerge and pass between fields again, while remaining under a covering of trees.

④ About 30 yards *before* the next wood,

Stagenhoe Park

go through a gap on the right and almost immediately left through another. Turn right in the field there and follow its edge as it curves round to the left and runs parallel to a drive to Stagenhoe Park. When adjacent to the Park's entrance gates the right of way coincides with the drive. Stay with the drive for 50 yards and turn right at a T-junction, where there is a tennis court at the corner.

⑤ After passing an attractive lodge house in a shallow dip, ignore a branch on the right and go gradually uphill, with a field on the left and a wood on the right. At the top of the hill there is a branch going off to the left, with a brick wall enclosing a corner. Ignore that branch and continue forward a few yards to a signposted path on the right. Initially unseen, this path runs under a line of trees, with fields on either side.

⑥ Soon enter a wood and in due course go right then left along the well-used path.

You should then find yourself following a shallow ditch on your right. On leaving the wood at a kissing-gate you have the prospect of a succession of three right-hand field edges each separated by kissing-gates, with Whitwell and its water tower in view ahead. Once in the final field you should go into the far right-hand corner and turn left there, walking along the field edge to another gate on the right 100 yards before the corner.

⑦ Turn left from that final kissing-gate and go forward just 20 yards to a T-junction. Turn right there and go downhill under trees, soon arriving back in Whitwell.

PLACES OF INTEREST NEARBY
The **Waterhall Farm and Craft Centre** in Whitwell is of interest to adults and children alike. Its tea room would be a pleasant place in which to end your day! The farm is open at weekends and school holidays from 10 am to 5 pm (4 pm in winter). Telephone: 01438 871256.

Aston
The Rose & Crown

MAP: OS EXPLORER 193 (GR 274227)   **WALK 9**   **DISTANCE:** 3¼ MILES

DIRECTIONS TO START: IF APPROACHING FROM THE A1(M) JUNCTION 7 TAKE THE A602 AND GO FORWARD OVER A SERIES OF ROUNDABOUTS FOR 2½ MILES TO BRAGBURY END; THEN TURN LEFT INTO ASTON LANE OPPOSITE THE VAN HAGE GARDEN CENTRE. CONTINUE FOR 1 MILE TO STRINGERS LANE AND TURN LEFT AT THE VILLAGE CROSSING IN ASTON FOR THE ROSE & CROWN. **PARKING:** IN THE PUB'S CAR PARK. ROADSIDE PARKING MAY BE POSSIBLE IN STRINGERS LANE NEAR THE START OF THE WALK.

It would be easy to miss the simple delights of this village while driving through on the way to Benington and the well-known Lordship Gardens. Here at Aston there are picturesque cottages, attractive public houses and superb views across the valley of the river Beane.

The walk commences with a dramatic descent to the river. It follows the waterside for over a mile before climbing steeply out of the valley and pursuing a near-straight course back to Aston.

The Rose & Crown

I'm sure you will share the sentiments I experienced when I first stepped inside the Rose & Crown – a truly delightful village hostelry excelling in comfort, orderliness, cleanliness and atmosphere! And that's a real credit to the history of the pub, which dates back at least to the beginning of the 19th century.

The food menu is notable in that it will not embarrass the leanest of pockets. Starting with the homemade soup you could go on to the pizza, cottage pie, omelettes or burgers – or something from the daily specials board. Sandwiches are well represented, as are vegetarian dishes. If watching your weight you could concentrate on the 'Calorie Conscious' items, which include tuna salad and filled jacket potatoes. If not, you could attempt the 'all day breakfast' – a really good fry-up!

Return here in the evening for more substantial offerings – steaks, mixed grill, chicken Kiev and a varied choice of desserts – or on Sunday for the two-course roast lunch. MacMullen's ales are available here; also special presentations – Winter's Tale for example.

Families are very welcome, evidenced by the pub's Children's Certificate and the children's menu. In winter enjoy the ambience of the real open fires, and in summer the pleasant garden with its pétanque pitch and its children's play area. The Rose & Crown is open 'all day, every day' Telephone: 01438 880243.

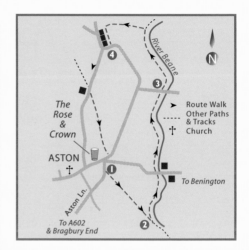

The Walk

① Go left along the road from the Rose & Crown and turn right at the junction into Stringers Lane; then join a path between houses on the left after 150 yards. This is opposite a timber barn and where the road curves to the right. The path soon places you in a level field, which you should cross straight on. When this in turn links you to another, larger, field, you should continue straight on and downhill to the far left-hand corner.

② On arrival at the corner, you should turn sharp hairpin left (almost doubling back, you are sure to say!) and follow the field edge, with the river immediately to your right. When the river snakes round to the right you should keep straight on across the field to a stile, and straight on again across a long narrow field to a road. With the river bridge and a farm to your right, cross the road and continue following the river to the next road, where you have the novelty of a working ford!

③ Stay with the river through two more

The river Beane almost hidden from view by the summer foliage

to the left to follow the next field edge to a stile near the far left-hand corner. After crossing the stile pass behind a row of houses along a right-hand field edge and soon join a road, Brookfield Lane.

④ Turn right along the road and soon left at the junction into Aston End Road; then look for a footpath leaving the road on the left after ¹/₃ mile. This is opposite a house numbered 93 and another footpath. Entering a field here you will then have another field followed by a fenced path, all taking you in a straight line parallel to the Beane valley. On meeting a recreation field – with its attendant children's play area – continue forward to a pavement and forward again to a cul-de-sac and a path between houses. Turn right at the road ahead and soon arrive back at the Rose & Crown – unless you prefer the Pig and Whistle nearby!

fields until, after a distance of ¹/₂ mile (measured from the previous road) you meet a waymarked uphill path. This is at the far end of the second field. Go uphill along the path, leaving the river behind and following a hedge on the right. Go forward over a stile at the top of the hill; then veer

> ### PLACES OF INTEREST NEARBY
> A visit to **Benington Lordship Gardens** is an absolute must in at least two seasons of the year – when the snowdrops are in bloom and when the summer borders are at their best. The approach from Aston is along Benington Road, not surprisingly! For opening times telephone: 01438 869668.

Braughing
The Axe and Compasses

DIRECTIONS TO START: FROM THE A1(T) ½ MILE NORTH OF THE PUCKERIDGE TURN-OFF, JOIN THE B1368 AND TURN FIRST OR SECOND RIGHT AFTER CROSSING THE OLD RAILWAY BRIDGE. THE SECOND TURN WILL TAKE YOU THROUGH BRAUGHING'S FORD – AN EXPERIENCE YOU MAY ENJOY! **PARKING:** IN THE PUB'S CAR PARK OR IN THE SQUARE OPPOSITE.

This attractive village has certain features that other villages might envy: two pubs, an excellent post office and general store, a picturesque ford – and the famous Braughing Sausage!

Its other cherished possession – community spirit – is exampled in the annual wheelbarrow race and in the celebration of Old Man's Day, of which more later.

The walk takes us easily to the summit of Pentlow Hill, where there are views as fine as any in East Hertfordshire. It follows the course of the river Quin and returns to the Square along Fleece Lane (a lovely village footpath) and through St Mary's churchyard.

The Axe and Compasses

The Axe and Compasses is well integrated into village life with its support for the local cricket team and darts championships – as well as the annual wheelbarrow race! On the food front it presents an impressive choice of starters, salads, main dishes, fish dishes, sandwiches, filled jacket potatoes and desserts. Chicken is free range, and sausages are the highly-esteemed locally-made variety. The latter are likely to come as 'wholegrain mustard roasted with cheese dumpling' or 'herb flavoured and stuffed with mushroom' – or the more familiar toad-in-the-hole. If, like me, you find the average helpings too daunting, you could opt for the 'senior citizens portions' from the same menu. Children may follow suit – and not be confined to fish fingers and the like! All this can be enjoyed at lunchtimes and evenings every day (Sunday lunch until 4pm).

Traditional opening hours are kept from Monday to Saturday, while on Sunday the pub is open from 12 noon to 10.30 pm. Around four real ales are offered, with Flowers IPA as standard. The pub likes to ring the changes with the other ales, which adds interest and enjoyment for the discerning customer. Telephone: 01920 821610

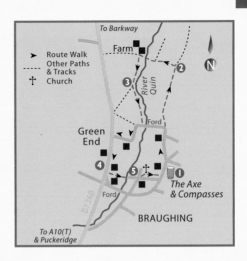

The Walk

① Go to the right on leaving the Axe and Compasses and soon branch half left by a small triangular green. Follow the road downhill and straight on to where it bends left. Leave the road at that point by crossing a brook and going forward on a track signposted to Bozen Green. The track takes you uphill and provides wide sweeping views of the Hertfordshire countryside – assuming your weather is kind, of course!

② Around the fields hereabouts there are grassy margins 'established by the landowner under the Countryside Stewardship Scheme for the benefit of wildlife'. Would that more landowners were like-minded! After 200 yards of level track turn left (that's the first branch since leaving the road) and go down another track to where it crosses the river Quin. Now you can choose between a path on the left just beyond the river or the cross-field path starting from a stile almost opposite farm buildings. The field path passes a single large tree at the halfway-point and meets up with the riverside path when adjacent to a wooded area.

③ Ignore the path going half right (diagonally and uphill) across the next field and go forward alongside the trees. You will have a view of Braughing's church spire directly ahead, while the river (which is initially under the trees) soon veers off to the left. On arrival at the road ahead you

The river Quin at Braughing.

will see the river down to the left, at a ford. Your route now is to turn right on the road, which you should follow between houses and 'farm' buildings around two turnings all the way to the B1368 road. Turn left at this and go as far as number '20', which was once the Golden Fleece Inn.

④ Opposite number 20 is 'D Whites, Butchers'. That such a small shop should be the source of the famous Braughing Sausage will be appreciated when you see the extensive buildings behind it. The sausage was 'invented' in 1954 and has become so popular that no less than 30,000 are now produced each week. Joined end to end that's two miles of sausage! Turning

left immediately beyond house number 20, you will find yourself on a footpath, Fleece Lane, where an event is recalled that is as memorable as the Braughing sausage is popular. In 1595 when Matthew Wall's coffin was being carried to the church, a bearer slipped on the wet leaves and the coffin fell to the ground. On hearing a knocking sound from within, they realised that Matthew was still alive, woken by the crash. When he died 'again' many years later his will provided for the sweeping of the lane, doubtless to prevent a recurrence of the event! The sweeping is now ceremoniously carried out by local schoolchildren each year on October 2nd.

⑤ On arrival at the crossing by St Mary's church you could go right along Church End to see the ford. This short diversion is included in your two miles, so don't be too alarmed at the prospect! Back at the church go into the churchyard and walk uphill through it to a gate at the far end. This will place you in the Square, with the Axe and Compasses in view ahead.

PLACES OF INTEREST NEARBY

Patmore Heath Nature Reserve is 3 miles east of Braughing. From the A120 between Bishop's Stortford and Standon, turn north from Little Hadham onto a minor road. A lane at the side of the Catherine Wheel pub leads into the reserve, which is rich in flora and insects as a result of its ponds and grass heathland habitat. This reserve is particularly special as areas of this type are ever-decreasing in the south-east, and has been designated a Site of Special Scientific Interest. It is open to the public all year round.

Dane End
The Boot

DIRECTIONS TO START: FROM THE A119 WHERE IT BYPASSES WATTON AT STONE, JOIN THE A602 AND TURN FIRST OR SECOND LEFT FOR DANE END (IF FIRST LEFT, TURN RIGHT AT THE NEXT ROAD JUNCTION). FROM THE A10(T) AT WARE APPROACH NORTH-WEST ALONG THE A602. **PARKING:** IN THE PUB'S CAR PARK OR ALONG EASINGTON ROAD NEARBY, WHERE THERE IS ALSO A SMALL PARKING AREA.

The largest settlement in Little Munden parish, Dane End is central to an attractive countryside of rolling hills, numerous small woodlands and working farms. Two watercourses – the Old Bourne and Dane End Tributary – cut through the parish, enhancing the scene. The latter is memorable in that it accompanies the main street and is overlooked by the Boot public house.

The walk commences by climbing the hill behind the village, heading for All Saints' church before crossing mostly level fields to Haultwick (pronounced 'Artic' by local people!). It returns to Dane End by way of the pleasant hamlet of Green End, enjoying expansive views in the process. The Rest & Welcome pub at Haultwick makes an ideal halfway house for the walk.

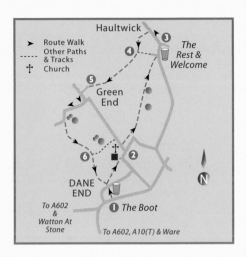

The Boot

The Boot was known as such way back in 1756, but has since been completely rebuilt. In recent years a barn at the rear of the premises was incorporated into the pub as an attractive dining room. The specials board is changed weekly and is likely to include such items as marrow stuffed with wild mushrooms and chicken jalfrezi (a curry). That's in addition to the more familiar pub fare. On Sunday the lunch menu consists of a roast – along with a vegetarian option. Prior booking for Sunday lunch is advisable. Meals are generally available throughout opening hours – until about 7 pm.

Carlsberg–Tetley real ale is available on a regular basis at the Boot. This is accompanied by a guest ale, which is changed weekly. The pub is open 'all day' from Tuesday to Sunday, but only in the evenings on Mondays (from 5 pm). Telephone: 01920 438770.

The Walk

① On leaving the front door of the Boot turn right and soon right again by Corner Cottage and Dane Cottage. Go through the pub's car park to its far side and walk straight on along a series of three short paths between the houses, crossing two roads in the process. On entering a field from a kissing-gate turn right and follow a flint wall for 25 yards to its midway point. Go half-left here and climb the field path towards the church and school at the top. Turning left along the road there, soon pass both the school and the church.

② Turn left at the road junction immediately beyond the church and leave the road for a path on the right after 50 yards. Follow the right-hand edge of the field – with a hedge on the right – all the way to a stile at the far end, descending a dip in the field as you proceed. Go half-left in the next field, aiming for a kissing-gate halfway along its opposite border. Maintaining the same direction, cross the next, triangular-shaped field to its sharp corner at the far end. Beyond a kissing-gate there you will pass to the left of a small wood along a thoughtfully unploughed fieldside path. Continue straight on along the next field path (which you may find *has* been ploughed!) to a road beyond the far right-hand corner. Go forward along the road to the junction by the Rest & Welcome pub.

③ From the Rest & Welcome turn left by the triangular green and walk along the road (in the Wood End direction) to a path on the left after 200 yards. This is opposite an attractively pargeted house, The Bell, formerly Haultwick's second public house. After passing between hedges, the path

The pub at Haultwick, halfway round the walk

enters a field and goes forward alongside a fence to a kissing-gate at the far end. Having entered another field from the kissing-gate, turn left and aim for a stile and hedge gap about 75 yards from the field's top left-hand corner.

④ Go through the gap and enter another field; then turn right immediately and follow the right-hand edge of this and the next field, with hedges on the right and houses in view ahead. Where the second field edge curves left around a pond, enter the right-hand meadow and cross this to a stile midway along the far side. This will place you on Green End's cricket ground where you should aim for the opposite right-hand corner.

⑤ From the cricket ground turn left into a rough drive and left at the road junction ahead. Turning right at the next junction by Yew Tree Cottage, soon pass a house that reminds us that it was once a pub – the Red Lion. Stay on the road as it passes a pond and turns left from a small triangular green; then leave the road very soon at the second (right-hand) bend. Keep forward here on a grassy bank and pass between a copse and a fenced field, shortly emerging at a field corner. Go straight on along the field edge and stay with it when it eventually turns half-left.

⑥ At a meeting of paths lower down (with a wood over to the left) turn right and cross the field downhill towards Dane End. Going briefly left at the bottom, rejoin that series of three short paths that we used at the start of the walk. After entering the pub's car park turn left at the road for the pub itself.

Codicote
The Goat

MAP: OS EXPLORER 182 (GR 217183)

WALK 12

DISTANCE: 2¼ MILES

DIRECTIONS TO START: FROM THE A1(M) AT JUNCTION 6 JOIN THE NORTH-GOING A1000, WELWYN DIRECTION (NOT WELWYN GARDEN CITY), THEN TURN LEFT INTO THE B656 FOR CODICOTE. **PARKING:** IN THE PUB'S CAR PARK OR ALONG THE HIGH STREET.

This busy work-a-day village retains remnants of an earlier age when its high street formed part of the Great North Road. Old cottages are there to be admired, along with the Goat and the Globe public houses and the former George and Dragon Inn; but the glory of this piece of Hertfordshire must surely lie in the valley to the south-west: the lovely river Mimram.

The walk loops westward from the village and runs parallel to the Mimram for ¼ mile. Should this prove tantalisingly short for your liking, there is an opportunity to explore the river valley further, before completing the walk. With Codicote raised above the surrounding countryside, there are good views to be enjoyed in several places along the route.

The Goat

One of three surviving hostelries in Codicote, the Goat can trace its existence back to at least 1754, when it was described as an alehouse. Its ancient roots are still reflected in its appearance – low oak beams within, timber framing without. Today the Goat is very much a community pub, supporting local institutions and charities. And it is even a venue for harvest thanksgiving services!

The pub is as homely in its cooking as in its welcome. Examples from its blackboard menu – which changes daily – are beef and ale pie, Thai chicken curry, Brie and broccoli pithivier. For a lighter touch you could opt for a ploughman's; for something spicy hot you could consider an item from the long list of balti dishes.

Meals are served at lunchtimes and, subject to prior booking, in the evenings. The pub is open for drinking 'all day, every day'. Telephone: 01438 820475.

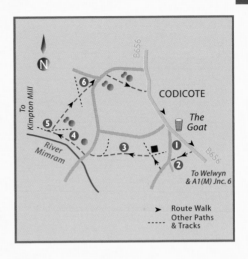

The Walk

① Go left along the High Street from the Goat and look for a footpath signpost on the right (it may not be obvious) after about 250 yards. This is opposite a petrol station and a short distance before a changed-use chapel. This will direct you onto a short drive (Dolimore Close) and beyond that to a tarmac path. Cross the cul-de-sac ahead and pass between houses to a recreation ground; then go forward along its right-hand edge to Cowards Lane at the far end.

② At the road junction with Cowards Lane cross over the small triangular green and go forward along the road ahead, maintaining your previous direction. After 100 yards or so leave the road and join a signposted path on the right. This passes between bungalows and soon meets a kissing-gate at a field corner. Go straight on along the field's left-hand edge, aiming for a stile in the far left-hand corner, with a school in view ahead. Having crossed the stile go left onto a tarmac path and, ignoring a turning on the right almost immediately, leave the tarmac for a fenced path backing onto gardens.

③ You will eventually lose the gardens as the path runs between fences and fields. A stile at the end of this stretch is labelled 'Hertfordshire Way'. You now have a steep descent under trees to a gated private drive at the bottom. After crossing the drive and descending a flight of steps, continue forward but now on a level path and with a field in view to your left. On meeting a road go left along this for 75 yards to a track on the right; but before you join this you could continue forward a short distance and be rewarded with a most pleasant view of the river Mimram. Back at

A fenced path en route

the track, this is signposted 'Kimpton Mill ¾' and runs uphill at first, with a wooded slope rising to the right and the river (seen best in winter) down to the left.

④ When confronted by a farm gate ahead (through which the hard track runs into a field) go a touch to the right and continue forward as before, while remaining under the trees. Our walk along this lovely river valley concludes all too soon – just where the wood on the right terminates and where a path runs hairpin right uphill. However, you could well continue the pleasure by keeping forward along the valley, perhaps for the ⅓ mile to Kimpton Mill, and returning by the same route.

⑤ Back at the wood, turn hairpin right (half-left if returning from Kimpton Mill) and go uphill through the trees, but for 75 yards only. Turn left from a waymark post at that point and head up to a stile, which is preceded by a short flight of steps. Go half-right from that stile and continue to another stile, which reveals a large field

ahead. Now you should cross this and the next two fields straight on (continuing your previous direction) towards the left-hand extremity of a distant wood. Of the two stiles giving entry to the third field, the right-hand of the two is the one you need ('Hertfordshire Way'). On arrival near the wood end go over a stile and pass under trees to a road.

⑥ Turn left along the road (not *across* it) and soon right at a T-junction; then go through a kissing-gate on the right after 50 yards. After a short stretch under trees another gate will place you at the start of a wide fenced path. Beyond three more gates the path joins the B656 road, by North Lodge. Turn right here and soon arrive back in Codicote High Street.

PLACES OF INTEREST NEARBY

The remains of a **Roman bathhouse** were excavated at Welwyn during the 1960s and 70s on the route of the present A1(M) road. These have been preserved under the embankment and can be viewed by the public. Telephone: 01707 271362 for details.

Datchworth
The Tilbury

DIRECTIONS TO START: FROM JUNCTION 6 OF THE A1(M) JOIN THE NORTH-GOING A1000 (WELWYN DIRECTION INITIALLY – *NOT* WELWYN GARDEN CITY), FOLLOWED BY THE NORTH-GOING B197, KNEBWORTH DIRECTION. WHEN THE B197 TURNS LEFT BY THE CHEQUERS INN, WOOLMER GREEN, TURN RIGHT INTO MARDLEYBURY ROAD FOR DATCHWORTH. THE PUB IS AT THE FAR END OF UPPER GREEN. **PARKING:** IN THE PUB'S CAR PARK OR ALONGSIDE UPPER GREEN.

Not far from some of Hertfordshire's busiest highways, this village and its surroundings retains much of its rural atmosphere and attractiveness – in its greens, its woodland and its arable fields. Datchworth itself is the archetypal English village, where cricket is played on the green and where the locals enjoy a pint at the pub.

Few walks as short as this can boast such variety of access – Roman road, byway, footpath, country lane, 'road used as a public path', village green. It has them all! In addition to this there are wide panoramic views and lovely woodland ponds.

The Tilbury

Also known as the Inn off the Green, the Tilbury once had a subtly different name – the Inn *on* the Green! Whether it is on or off is of little consequence, I would have thought; what is certain is that the pub's reputation for food is acknowledged far and wide.

The Tilbury's speciality is its home-made pies, of which there are around 20 varieties. There is also a very impressive choice of starters and main meals, including a good number of vegetarian dishes. Added to this are filled jacket potatoes, sandwiches, burgers, ploughman's and sweets. The Tilbury is also well known for its ales, in particular the landlord's very own brews – Five Hides and Hop Pit! Equally intriguing names appear on the blackboard, such as Dark Horse Deathwish and Eccleshall Oblivion!

In summer the garden is a nice place to enjoy all this good living, while contemplating the pastoral view across the fields. The pub is open 'all day, every day' and meals are available every lunchtime and evening except Mondays. The Plough opposite has the same restriction; so keep this walk for a different day! Telephone: 01438 812496.

The Walk

① When leaving the Tilbury go left immediately at the crossing into Watton Road, which is signposted to Watton at Stone. Leave the road after 250 yards by joining a track on the right just prior to the first road junction. The track is labelled 'Public byway 19' and runs a straight course between fields. Stay on the track (ignoring

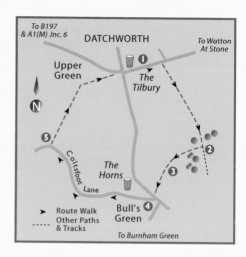

branching footpaths) until you find yourself in a shallow dip adjacent to a pond and just inside Bramfield Woods.

② Turn right from a waymark post and pass immediately to the left of this long pond – which may be dry! On arrival at the far end of the pond bear right and climb a few steps to a field. Turn left and follow the left-hand field edge, soon passing another pond (on the left – and more likely to be wet!) and ignoring a path to the right. The tall trees that accompany the pond give way to a scrubby hedge, and a gap in the hedge after a few yards reveals a kissing-gate. This is where the field edge pulls out of an S-curve.

③ The stile places you in the sharp corner of another field. Keep more or less to the left-hand side of this and the next field and aim for a kissing-gate to the right of a shingle-tiled house (wooden tiles on walls and roof). If in doubt take guidance from overhead wires as they head in the same direction. You may have caught a glimpse of the Horns pub as you walked through

The village green

that field. You will see it more fully when you soon join the road at Bull's Green.

④ Cross the road to Coltsfoot Lane opposite and soon commence a very pleasant half mile amble along this quiet country road. When you pass Coltsfoot Country Retreat (formally Coltsfoot Farm) you will agree that it is well placed! Included in the view from further along the lane is the spire of Datchworth church, which is situated at the northern end of the village.

⑤ When you are about midway between the second labelled passing-place and the lowest point of the lane, leave the lane for a RUPP on the right – a Road used as a Public Path, but simply a track to us! Its signpost is set well off the lane and may be easily missed. The track runs between hedgerow trees and fields, passes a recreation ground and finally emerges on Datchworth's Upper Green – where there are seats on which to relax and enjoy the scene. The Tilbury will be found beyond the far end of the green.

PLACES OF INTEREST NEARBY

Knebworth House and Country Park are situated 2½ miles north-west of Datchworth – as the crow flies. There is something for all ages there – the house itself, the gardens (including a herb garden), a children's playground, a Children's Room in the house, a maze and numerous special events. You could drive there by way of Woolmer Green and Knebworth. Telephone: 01438 812661. **Tewin Orchard** is two miles to the south and can be approached by way of Bull's Green and Burnham Green. See Walk 19 (Tewin) for details.

Much Hadham
The Old Crown

DIRECTIONS TO START: MUCH HADHAM IS ON THE B1004 ABOUT 4 MILES WEST OF THE CENTRE OF BISHOP'S STORTFORD. THE OLD CROWN IS EASILY FOUND AT THE SOUTHERN END OF THE VILLAGE AT HADHAM CROSS. **PARKING:** IN THE PUB'S SMALL CAR PARK OR ALONG THE ROADSIDE NEARBY.

Much Hadham is thought to possess the longest village high street in the country. Approaching one mile in length, it contains many architectural gems – from humble cottages to superior houses. Below the village lies the river Ash, adding beauty and charm to the pastures through which it flows.

On leaving the Old Crown we descend to these pastures and follow them northwards through the valley. Rejoining High Street we soon leave it for the fields to the west, and there enjoy an impressive view of Moor Place, a large 18th century mansion overlooking the village.

The Old Crown

The much-used adage 'small is beautiful' applies without reservation to this delightful free house where the proprietors maintain a tradition going back at least to the 1850s. For many years the selling of beer went hand in hand with a bakery. Today it goes hand in hand with the provision of good home-cooked food!

Under the 'light meals and starters' heading, the regular menu offers filled jacket potatoes, ploughman's, sandwiches and other snacks including Old Crown Combo – 'a selection of potato skins, onion rings and tiger prawns in filo pastry'. 'Main courses' include the locally famous Braughing sausages, Old Crown pies, supreme of chicken, steaks and vegetarian dishes. Fresh fish is available at lunchtimes on Thursday to Saturday. For further choices you are referred to the daily specials board, which includes a selection of desserts. Children have their own small menu, so they are obviously welcome here! On Sunday a traditional roast is offered along with the bar menu. For the roast lunch, you will need to book in advance. In addition to four real ales, there are several wines, and house wines by the glass.

The pub is open at the traditional hours from Monday to Thursday and 'all day' Friday to Sunday. Meals are available at lunchtimes and in the evenings from Monday to Saturday and 'all day' Sunday (until 8 pm). There is a patio at the front, although no garden as such. Telephone: 01279 842753.

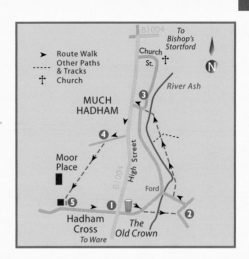

The Walk

① Turn right when you leave the Old Crown and go along the High Street for about 100 yards to a path by the Congregational church. This path runs downhill between fences to a road at the bottom. Turn right there and left after 20 yards through a gate. Follow the right-hand field edge half-left with respect to the road. Cross the river Ash at the far end of the field and continue forward in the next field to a kissing-gate on the right. This is three-quarters of the way along the field edge and connects with a road.

② Turn left along the road and soon left again at a road junction. When halfway down this road go through a kissing-gate on the right (or continue along the road if you wish to see the ford; and then come back). Cross the pasture here, almost at right angles to the road and aiming for a gate at the far end. The gate is a little to the right of the river Ash and places you in the next, much longer, pasture. From a kissing-gate at the far end go over a rough drive to another gate and yet another pasture. At

The 18th-century Moor Place seen on the walk

the far end of this third pasture cross a footbridge and walk a short grassy path to a road, at a bend.

③ Go left at the road and straight on to the High Street, opposite the Bull Inn. Turn left and walk along the High Street as far as the war memorial and go through the gates on the right just there. Ascending a drive, walk only as far as a cattle grid (130 yds), then cross to a stile on the left.

④ You now have a sequence of fields to cross in the direction slightly left of a distant farm complex. In the process you will pass a cattle trough in mid-field while enjoying a superb view of 'the big house', Moor Place. The house dates back to 1776 and has been in the same family (the Normans) since the 1880s. Purchase of this fine house was doubtless made possible through the family's involvement in the West Indies sugar trade. After passing the

farm complex keep more or less straight on, aiming for the right-hand extremity of a stand of trees. On leaving the fields keep forward over a crossing of drives and pass to the left of Dell Cottage. A kissing-gate and a short flight of steps beyond the house will lead you down to a road.

⑤ All that remains is to turn left along the road and walk back down to Hadham Cross and the Old Crown.

PLACES OF INTEREST NEARBY

No need to go very far to fill the remainder of your day: along the High Street is the excellent **Forge Cottage Museum** which includes a Victorian kitchen garden and a working blacksmith's shop. It is open Friday to Sunday and bank holidays from 11 am to 5 pm (or dusk). Telephone: 01279 843301. Further along **Hopleys** beautiful 4 acre garden and nursery is open daily except Tuesday from March to October.

Ayot St Lawrence
The Brocket Arms

MAP: OS EXPLORER 182 (GR 195168)

WALK 15

DISTANCE: 1¾ MILES

DIRECTIONS TO START: FROM WHEATHAMPSTEAD TAKE THE B653 IN THE WELWYN DIRECTION AND TURN FIRST LEFT IN LESS THAN ¼ MILE. TURN FIRST LEFT AGAIN AFTER A FURTHER ¾ MILE. IT'S THEN ANOTHER ¾ MILE TO AYOT ST LAWRENCE.
PARKING: SINCE THE BROCKET ARMS DOES NOT HAVE A CAR PARK, YOU WILL NEED TO LEAVE YOUR CAR ALONG THE ROADSIDE NEARBY OR ELSEWHERE IN THE VILLAGE. PARKING WOULD DOUBTLESS BE EASIER ON WEEKDAYS THAN AT WEEKENDS, ESPECIALLY IN SUMMER.

I think even Bernard Shaw would be surprised at how little the immediate countryside around his chosen village has changed since his day. Progress there certainly has been, but, apart from the ubiquitous motor car, you could well imagine yourself back in the first half of the 20th century as you walk the paths hereabouts.

Circulating around Ayot St Lawrence along trackways and field paths this short walk includes a close pass of Ayot Manor House and the 'new' St Lawrence church. In the village itself is the old church – now a ruin – and Shaw's Corner, Bernard Shaw's home from 1906 until his death in 1950.

The Brocket Arms

A pub more steeped in history and atmosphere could hardly be imagined! With the huge inglenook fireplace in the bar ablaze with logs, this is the place to be after a winter walk. You can even sit in the chimney space itself for a really good toasting! And that's just one of three open fires (one of which is gas lit) to greet you when you arrive for the serious business of eating and drinking.

You would also do well to come to Ayot St Lawrence on a nice summer's day, especially when Shaw's Corner is open (Wednesday–Sunday). You will then have two gardens to enjoy – the pub's and Bernard Shaw's!

The lunchtime menu 'on the black-board' is good traditional pub fare: soup, fish, homemade quiche, macaroni cheese, chilli con carne, curry, steak and kidney pie, game pie. There is also a choice of ploughman's and salads, and a range of desserts which are homemade. All this can be taken in the bars or the dining room. Come back of an evening and choose from a more extensive restaurant menu.

Meals are served every lunchtime (until 2.30 pm) and evening except Monday and Sunday evenings. The pub is however open 'all day, every day', plenty of time to imbibe one of the five traditional ales, the lagers or the cider. In addition, comfortable accommodation is offered all year round – from single rooms to rooms with four posters! Telephone: 01438 820250 (www.brocketarms.com).

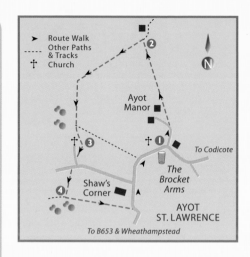

The Walk

① Go to the right after leaving the Brocket Arms and join a tarmac drive on the left when the road soon turns right. The drive is an entrance to Ayot Manor House, as well as a bridleway. When the drive curves left on its way to Ayot House (this is not the Manor House) keep forward through a gateway to a gravel track. The Manor House itself comes into view very soon, through a hedge-gap on the left. Although Tudor in origin, the Manor House was modified late in the 17th century, which explains its present appearance. Keep straight on along the track.

② Where the track turns right by Abbotshay Farm, a footpath sign beckons you into a field corner on the left – the second field corner just here, not the first. Follow the left-hand edge of the field, where tall trees divide the fields, to a stile in the far left-hand corner. The attractive view to your right is over the valley to the east of Kimpton. Once over the stile walk across the meadow towards Ayot St Lawrence 'new' church, notable by its columned front. That's half-right if your back is to the stile.

Shaw's Corner, Bernard Shaw's home, now in the care of the National Trust

The fact that the church was built to impress onlookers can be understood even today. When built in the late 1700s to the design of Nicholas Revett, it would be thought of as very progressive and fashionable.

③ A stile is followed immediately by a churchyard gate directly ahead. Passing in front of the church soon bear right through a five-bar gate and follow the church drive when it curves left. The church parking space will be in view over to your right. On arrival at a road turn right and go over a stile on the left very soon – just beyond Prior's Holt. Walk along the left-hand edge of the field to a stile in the far left-hand corner. A few steps down followed by a few yards forward will place you at a T-junction in the path, with a wood just ahead.

④ Turn left and, with the wood to your right at the start, soon go forward between fences and fields. The path terminates at a bend in a road. Go left and uphill in the road by Shaw's Corner – the house where Bernard Shaw lived for 44 years. Keep straight on from the road junction (or left for Shaw's house) and follow the road round to the Brocket Arms, passing the old church as you go. In the late 1700s the lord of the manor Sir Lionel Lyde started to dismantle the church but was stopped in his tracks by the Bishop. Hence the church's ruinous state. Sir Lionel's reasoning was that it would spoil the view from his house; and in any case he was building a replacement – the church we saw earlier.

PLACES OF INTEREST NEARBY

Shaw's house and garden are cared for by the National Trust and are open on Wednesday to Sunday (and bank holiday) afternoons from mid-March to October inclusive. A visit to the house is always a memorable experience, while the garden is particularly beautiful and well worth seeing.

Gustard Wood
The Cross Keys

MAP: OS EXPLORER 182 (GR 175165)	WALK 16	DISTANCE: 2½ MILES

DIRECTIONS TO START: THE CROSS KEYS IS ON THE B651 MIDWAY BETWEEN WHEATHAMPSTEAD AND KIMPTON. IF DRIVING NORTH FROM WHEATHAMPSTEAD TAKE CARE TO TURN RIGHT WITH THE B651 AFTER 1¼ MILES. **PARKING:** IN THE PUB'S CAR PARK OR ALONG THE ROADSIDE.

The region around which our walk circulates owes much of its attractiveness to the estate of Lamer House. There are pleasant pastures and unspoilt woodland, and a truly magnificent avenue of lime trees. It is charming in the same way as its nearby neighbour, Ayot St Lawrence, with which it seems to have an affinity.

The walk forms an almost perfect triangle: outward alongside pastures and woodland; then through the avenue of lime trees and along the drive to Lamer Park Farm; finally in a gentle incline through Lamer Wood.

The Cross Keys

You could hardly imagine a pub in a more attractive and peaceful location – surrounded as it is by fields and woodland, and close to a quiet country road. In summer the large garden takes full advantage of its rural setting, while in winter the cosy atmosphere of the pub's interior is sheer delight! The warmth of the marvellous inglenook fireplace is echoed in the warmth offered to all-comers, including walkers, cyclists and families.

Food is served every lunchtime and from Wednesday to Saturday evenings. Included are fish dishes (scampi, plaice and trout), macaroni cheese, filled jacket potatoes, ploughman's, sandwiches and salads. There are sausages and there are BMTs – bacon, mushroom and tomato in fried bread. Examples from the sweets menu are lemon meringue pie, apple crumble and Alabama chocolate fudge cake. On Sundays the choice is between sandwiches and one of the landlord's special dishes (he is 'cook' on that day!); so come prepared for something different. There are two very pleasant dining rooms away from the bar, ideal for families. As always, it is well worth booking a table if calling for Sunday lunch.

The Cross Keys is a free house and keeps a range of around six real ales. There is also a good choice of lagers and wines. Traditional pub hours are kept except for the 'all day' opening on summer Sundays and the possible extended opening on summer Saturdays. Telephone: 01582 832165.

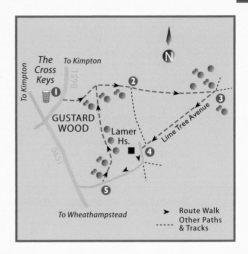

The Walk

① Go left in the road (the B651) as soon as you leave the pub's car park and cross to a signposted path opposite. This is adjacent to a tall brick wall and soon leads to a stile. A long fenced path takes you forward between a field and the wall and terminates at another stile. Passing a cattle trough and byre at the start, follow a fence towards the left-hand corner of a wood. Go forward alongside the next two field edges, with a wire fence to your left along the second field and the wood on your immediate right all the way.

② On reaching the far end of the wood turn right to a stile and enter a long narrow field. Turn left immediately in the field and soon cross another stile. This places you at the start of a wide grassy margin bordered by trees on the left and pastures on the right. Stay with this all the way to a stile at the far end (there is an intervening stile along the way), a total distance approaching ½ mile. On arrival you will immediately meet a crossing, with trees directly ahead.

③ Turn very sharp right at the crossing

The drive to Lamer House

and enter a magnificent avenue of lime trees. This leads to Lamer House – which we will see later – and provides some fine views over the Lea valley and beyond. The avenue is very nearly ½ mile in length and punctuated by a stile along its route and another at the far end. The latter connects with a tarmac drive to Lamer Park Farm.

④ Turn left into the drive and stay with it as it curves left, then right, ignoring a footpath leaving from the left and a track going forward. As you progress along the drive an excellent view is to be had of Lamer House though a gap in its very fine hedge. The house was once owned by Apsley Cherry-Garrard, a member of Captain Scott's second expedition to Antarctica and author of *The Worst Journey in the World*. Lamer Wood takes over from the hedge as the drive runs downhill.

⑤ Leave the drive about 30 yards prior to its lowest point and cross a stile on the right leading into the wood. The path runs through the wood for about ½ mile, meandering and turning left at one point, then turning right to resume its former direction. Fields come into view and a stile takes you further forward. A wide pit is passed (on your right) and the path finally meets the light of day, at a stile. Cross another stile on the left immediately and find yourself in the field that you trod earlier. All that now remains is to follow a right-hand fence to a stile beyond a cattle trough and horse byre, and to follow the fenced path back to the B651 and the Cross Keys.

> **PLACES OF INTEREST NEARBY**
> **Wheathampstead** is an attractive little town on the river Lea 1¼ miles south of Gustard Wood. A little further south lies **Nomansland Common**, a pleasant, largely open heathland. A car park is provided ¼ mile off the B651.

Wilstone
The Half Moon

MAP: OS EXPLORER 181 (GR 904142)   **WALK 17**   **DISTANCE:** 3¼ MILES

DIRECTIONS TO START: FROM THE DUAL A41 ROUNDABOUT ½ MILE WEST OF TRING, FOLLOW THE B4009 (NOT THE A41!) FOR ½ MILE ONLY; THEN KEEP AHEAD FOR 1 MILE TO ASTON CLINTON. TURN RIGHT THERE (MARSWORTH DIRECTION) ONTO THE B489 AND LEFT FOR WILSTONE AFTER 1½ MILES. **PARKING:** IN THE PUB'S CAR PARK OR ALONG THE ROADSIDE NEARBY.

This quiet unassuming village lies within the watery orbit of the Grand Union Canal, its branches and its sustaining reservoirs. Originally constructed to provide water to the summit level of the canal, these reservoirs perform an additional function, that of havens and breeding sites for an impressive variety of birds and waterfowl. Come here in winter if you wish to see the ducks and geese in their greatest numbers.

The walk circumnavigates Wilstone Reservoir, partly along its embankment, partly through nearby fields. It includes a short diversion to a bird hide and a stretch of the Wendover Canal, long defunct but now being reinstated. Allow extra time for the walk; bring binoculars; enjoy this delightful place to the full!

The Half Moon

This could be the house where, in 1622, the alehouse keeper was fined for selling beer on a Sunday! No such restrictions or accusations today, where the friendly licensees keep a very popular village pub. The atmosphere and comfort is matched by an appetising choice of meals. There is a wide choice of well-established dishes – steak pie, cod fillet, farmhouse ham, tuna pasta bake, for example. For a less demanding snack you could choose from filled jacket potatoes, sandwiches, bean-burgers or 'chickwich' – chicken in crispy batter in a bap, with salad. In addition to the regular menu there is a daily specials board and a sweets menu. Food is available every lunchtime and evening with the exception of Monday evening. Families are made very welcome in the dining room; and children can enjoy their own special menu.

There is a good choice of ales – Adnam's Best Bitter, Flower's Original, Bass and Tetley Bitter.

The pub keeps traditional opening hours every day. Telephone: 01442 826410.

The Walk

① Turn left on leaving the Half Moon and, passing the village stores, take the left-hand branch in the road – New Road. Stay in this no through road to its far end, not omitting to admire the fine brickwork of the '1907' houses and the one-time '1837' chapel. Go through the gate at the road end and immediately through another gate on the right. This gives access to a field, which you should cross diagonally to another gate near the furthest corner.

② On joining a road cross to a footpath a little to the right on the opposite side. A footbridge takes you over a brook and into a small field. Walking across this soon go over a farm track to a short path and another footbridge. Climb a stile on the left immediately and enter the left-hand field. Cross this diagonally, maintaining more or less your previous direction and joining the busy B489 from a stile in the far corner. Looking right along the road you will see a small car park. A safe approach to this is by a footpath beyond the roadside hedge opposite. Access to the path is achieved by crossing the road to a hedge-gap.

③ From the car park climb the flight of steps leading up to the reservoir's embankment. Go right along the embankment (the water on your left) and, on reaching its far corner, turn left under the trees, keeping company with the reservoir and ignoring a path leaving from the right.

④ When confronted by a meeting of paths and a nature reserve information board, you have the opportunity to visit a bird hide by

Wilstone Reservoir

soon under power lines and arriving at a field corner.

⑤ Turn right from the corner and follow a hedge on the left. Enter the next field and go forward to a waymark post in a shallow dip in the fields, with those power lines running parallel over to your right. Turn left to follow yet another hedge, with the field rising uphill to your right. Turn right from the far corner and follow a fence uphill to a short flight of steps at the top.

⑥ The steps will place you on a raised path, beyond which is the bed of the former Wendover Canal. Turn left along the raised path and stay with this for 350 yards to a footpath crossing. The Reservoir Trail goes off to the right here (over the 'canal') but we turn left and descend a path under shrubby trees. At the bottom of the hill turn right into a track and walk alongside tall trees. When the trees terminate don't continue forward (the track crosses the fields) but turn left towards a corner of the reservoir.

⑦ It's now a straightforward matter of walking on the embankment all the way back to the car park. After descending the steps there, go right along the roadside path and soon cross to Tring Road at the junction. You can now either walk along Tring Road back to the Half Moon (it's not far) or retrace the first part of this stroll. For the latter go through a gate just beyond New Road and cross the field diagonally to another gate in the opposite corner.

following a path on the left. Back at the information board you should go half-right (relative to your earlier direction) through a gap and over a stream into the right-hand of two fields, taking care to ignore a stile *before* the stream. As an aid to your navigation it is worth mentioning that our route now follows a series of left-hand field edges along a zig-zag route waymarked as the Tring Reservoir Trail. In due course we will leave the Reservoir Trail and make our way back to Wilstone.

Keeping company with the left-hand trees at the start, and in the same direction as overhead wires, aim for a stile in the hedge directly ahead. An electricity pole stands nearby. Cross a footbridge there and climb a few steps into the next field. Follow a deep ditch on the left as far as the field corner; then turn left (the ditch terminates here) to pass alongside the left-hand hedge,

---

PLACES OF INTEREST NEARBY
The Grand Union Canal at **Startop's End**, on the B489 in the Ivinghoe direction. Lots of boating interest there.

Flamstead
The Three Blackbirds

MAP: OS EXPLORER 182 (GR 078146) **WALK 18** **DISTANCE:** 2 MILES

DIRECTIONS TO START: FLAMSTEAD CAN BE ACCESSED FROM THE A5 AT FRIAR'S WASH – WEST OF JUNCTION 9 OF THE M1 MOTORWAY. JOIN CHEQUERS LANE FROM THE A5 AND DRIVE THE ½ MILE TO THE VILLAGE, IGNORING DELMEREND LANE AS YOU GO.
PARKING: IN THE PUB'S CAR PARK OR ALONG THE ROADSIDE NEARBY.

Who would guess that this peaceful unspoilt village is less than one mile from the M1 motorway? Among its architectural gems is the lovely terrace of almshouses opposite the Three Blackbirds. Equally prized are the wall paintings in the church. In the churchyard itself there is interest of a different kind – graves dating back to the plague of 1604.

The walk takes in the glorious panorama of Trowley Bottom, its southern slopes crowned with woodland. The tiny hamlet in Trowley Bottom is a delight, with its cottage terrace, its farm and its quiet country lanes.

The Three Blackbirds

Parts of this attractive pub go back 400 to 500 years, predating the almshouses opposite. In more recent times it existed under different labels – the Bird in Hand and the Blackbird. It is as attractive inside as out and maintains a comfortable welcoming ambience and there is a dining area where families are always welcome.

The menu card is changed daily, and includes starters, main dishes and puddings. Such delights as chicken breast and bacon in Dijon sauce, or salmon fillet in tarragon and lemon sauce might take your fancy; or you might prefer moussaka, steak and kidney pie or scampi, for example. For pudding you could choose, say, chocolate rum roulade and fresh cream, or Belgian ice cream. On Sundays the choice is between a traditional roast, a fish or a vegetarian dish – in addition to starters and sweets. But Sunday is a popular day here, so you are best advised to book your place!

The ales on offer usually include Adnam's Bitter, Courage Best and Spitfire!

The pub is open 'all day, every day' and meals are served at lunchtimes and evenings from Tuesday to Sunday, with the exception of Sunday evening. In the summer, benches and umbrellas are set up to convert the car park into a very pleasant dining area, where light meals are served. Telephone: 01582 840330.

The Walk

① From the Three Blackbirds go left into Trowley Hill Road and soon enter the churchyard. Passing just to the right of the

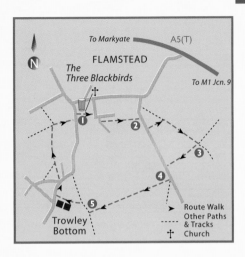

church, emerge from the far side through a gate near the right-hand corner. Turn right in the road there and follow this round to the left. Turn right very soon (into Pie Garden!) and join a footpath on the left running between gardens. This path is signposted 'Chiltern Way' and soon places you in a field corner – from a kissing-gate. Walk the left-hand edge of the field (the top edge) to the far corner, where you will find a short path leading to a road.

② Turn right at the road and follow it down for about 100 yards to a rough drive on the left, and soon leave this for a path under trees on the left. After a further 100 yards this path will place you in a field corner, from which you should continue forward – but for a short distance only. A stile on the left is your cue to turn right (*not* over the stile!) and to cross the very large field downhill. Hopefully other walkers will have gone before and you can follow in their footsteps. If not, you should aim for – but not climb – a stile in the bottom of the valley.

③ When at the bottom of the valley turn

Saunders almhouses in Flamstead

right to follow the field edge, alongside a fence on the left. You will be accompanied by a fenced track on the left; and after that you will join a road. Turn left at the road and go along this for 100 yards to a footpath on the right, opposite College Farm Stud. There is a bridleway leaving from the same point. This runs uphill and should be ignored!

④ The level footpath will take you along the right-hand edge of a field and, halfway along the field, through a gap on the right. Continuing in your previous direction, you will pass between a hedge and a fence – with fields on either side – and eventually arrive adjacent to the field corners. Continue forward again – to the left of a hedge now – and in due course meet a T-junction.

⑤ Turn right at the junction and go uphill on the well-made track, turning left with it higher up, while ignoring a path going

further uphill under trees. When the track turns left towards Trowley Bottom Farm keep straight on along a grassy path and shortly arrive in Trowley Bottom. After passing The Haven, a lovely terrace of cottages, bear right into White Hill (uphill) and turn left at a road junction. After only a few yards along this road join a footpath on the right and follow this up to a field corner, passing a meadow on the way. Go uphill from the corner along the right-hand field edge – for ³/₄ or more of its length – until you meet a crossing path. Turn right here and walk alongside gardens to Trowley Hill Road, then left along the road for the Three Blackbirds.

PLACES OF INTEREST NEARBY
The well-known **Whipsnade Wild Animal Park** is 5 miles to the north-west along the A5 via Markyate, followed by the B4540. Telephone: 01582 872171.

Tewin
The Rose & Crown

MAP: OS EXPLORER 182 (GR 272148)	WALK 19	DISTANCE: 3 MILES

DIRECTIONS TO START: TEWIN IS ONE MILE NORTH OF THE B1000 BETWEEN HERTFORD AND WELWYN. IF COMING FROM THE A1(M) JOIN THE A1000 (HERTFORD DIRECTION) AT JUNCTION 6. WHEN THE A1000 TURNS RIGHT AT DIGSWELL KEEP FORWARD INTO HERTFORD ROAD (DIGSWELL RAILWAY VIADUCT IN VIEW AHEAD); AND WHEN THE B1000 COMES IN FROM THE RIGHT KEEP FORWARD AGAIN AND TURN FIRST LEFT FOR TEWIN.
PARKING: IN THE PUB'S CAR PARK OR ALONG THE ROADSIDE BY LOWER GREEN.

At its heart Tewin is a pleasant unassuming village surrounded on all sides by attractive walking country. But what I take most delight in is the peaceful churchyard of St Peter's. High above the Mimram valley, this is the ideal place for quiet relaxation and contemplation.

The walk takes us on a complete circuit around the village, visiting St Peter's church in the process and enjoying fine views across the valley.

The Rose & Crown

The Rose & Crown is situated in the heart of the village and overlooks Lower Green. According to a potted history placed above the bar, it once formed part of a farm and was used for manorial court sessions.

The food here is very popular, with the lunchtime menu listing no less than 20 main courses, including steak, chicken and fish dishes, steak and ale pie, salmon and tarragon fish cakes and burgers 'n' mash. A number of sandwiches and burgers are offered, also puddings that you will find difficult to resist! In addition to a selection of real ales – including guest ales – there is an impressive variety of wines.

The pub is open 'all day, every day' and meals are served every lunchtime and evening. Telephone: 01438 717257.

The Walk

① You will find a public byway (Back Lane) immediately to the left of the Rose & Crown. This eventually turns right between fields and, much later, passes a pond on the right. When the byway soon meets Upper Green stay on the track as it curves round to the road.

② Turn right at the road and stay with it when it passes the Plume of Feathers and a road junction, Tewin Hill; then join a footpath on the left beyond house No. 74 when the road curves a little to the right. A few steps will place you on a path running between fences. From the end of this path a kissing-gate leads into the field ahead. Then turn right immediately, so that a fence is on your right. Now follow that fence, soon

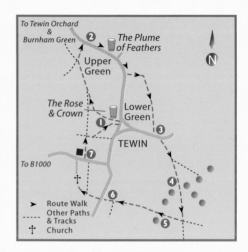

between fields and all the way to the trees in the far right-hand corner of the field. A path between gardens will then lead you out to a road.

③ Turn left and leave the road after 150 yards where it curves to the left. A footpath on the right here gives you access to a very large field, which you should cross towards the woodland opposite. If you aim for a point ¼ of the way from the left-hand end of the wood, that should be about right – but only until you are about halfway across. It is there that you should take the right-hand branch at a Y-junction, aiming now for a footbridge – initially unseen – leading into the wood.

④ Having entered the wood, go half-right uphill – not half left! The field that you have just left will then be in view down to your right. On arrival at the top of the wood ignore a branch on the right and enter a field at its corner, then strike across the field towards an avenue of lime trees at a point 5½ trees from its left-hand extremity! Although there is a kissing-gate

Lower Green, Tewin

on the left at that point you should turn right to pass under the avenue, with the Mimram valley in view down to your left.

⑤ Re-enter the wood from the far end of the avenue and go straight on down the slope, ignoring a branch on the right and assisted by two flights of steps. This will place you back in the field that you left earlier. Go straight on across the field, entering a dip near the start and aiming at St Peter's church, of which you may only see the spire. Keep forward when you meet a hedge (on the left) to a road.

⑥ Cross the road to a kissing-gate and pass between fences to another gate. Go in and out of the dip ahead and continue forward to the corner of St Peter's churchyard at the top. Walk through the churchyard to the drive on the far side. Notice the huge clock on the tower as you leave the church along

its drive, and on arrival at the far end of the drive turn right at the road.

⑦ Soon leave the road at a kissing-gate, just beyond a timber-framed building on the left; then progress along a fenced path to a gate at the far end. Turn right from the gate and walk along a field edge, with a hedge on the right and as far as a waymark post. Go half-left across the field here, cutting off a large corner and soon passing between a garden and a bowling green. At the road ahead turn left for the Rose & Crown.

PLACES OF INTEREST NEARBY

Tewin Orchard is just off the Burnham Green road ½ mile north of the village centre. It lies close to the walk near Upper Green. Originally planted in 1933, the orchard has been restored with traditional fruit varieties.

Wareside
The White Horse

MAP: OS EXPLORER 194 (GR 395155)   **WALK 20**   **DISTANCE:** 2½ MILES

DIRECTIONS TO START: WARESIDE IS 3 MILES FROM WARE ON THE B1004. THE WHITE HORSE IS EASILY FOUND ON THIS ROAD IN THE HEART OF THE VILLAGE. WARE ITSELF IS ACCESSIBLE FROM THE A10. **PARKING:** IN THE PUB'S CAR PARK. ROADSIDE PARKING IS OUT OF THE QUESTION UNLESS YOU DRIVE THE FIRST PART OF THE WALK AS FAR AS THE SCHOOL AND PARK ALONGSIDE THE GREEN THERE. FOR THIS GO ALONG THE ROAD SIGNPOSTED TO BABBS GREEN AND TURN LEFT AT THE T-JUNCTION.

Wareside is an attractive little village, and at its heart consists of a few cottages and two pubs. It is often a starting point for exploring the fields and meadows that accompany the river Ash to the south. There are, however, many quiet fields and bridleways to the north, where the walker can enjoy being 'away from it all'.

We explore a little of this by strolling along a lovely quiet lane from Reeves Green to Morley Ponds. Joining fieldside paths from the ponds we head north to Newhall Green and Legges Cottage, returning to Wareside through a series of fields and paddocks.

The White Horse

This pub manages to be all things to all people. The public bar is favoured by locals who call in for a pint and a game of pool or darts, while the lounge and restaurant are tailored for those arriving for a good meal in comfort and an old-world atmosphere – especially in winter when the huge inglenook fireplace is radiating its warmth.

The menus are many and all-embracing. Bar snacks range from soup, sandwiches and ploughman's to omelettes, scampi and haddock. For something more substantial the restaurant menu or the 'daily specials' board should be consulted for its extensive choice of starters, main courses and desserts. A roast lunch is available on Sundays, along with the restaurant and bar snacks menus, but prior booking is advised. The 'young customers' menu' is carefully thought out, with attention paid to both small and large appetites – from 'golden tiddlers' to 5oz sirloin steaks. In addition to Greene King real ales there is a good selection of wines, including house wines.

The pub is open at the traditional hours from Monday to Saturday and 'all day' on Sunday. Meals are available at lunchtimes and in the evenings everyday. If your dog is with you, he (or she) is welcome in the public bar or in the garden. Telephone: 01920 462582.

The Walk

① Cross over from the White Horse and join the road signposted to Babbs Green. This is midway between the White Horse and the Plough. After a few yards go left

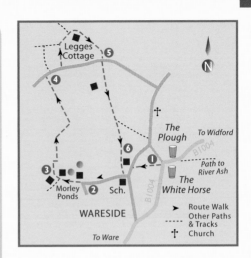

into a footpath immediately to the right of Bourne Cottage. This path is accompanied by a ditch – complete with water, perhaps – and takes you uphill to a road at the top. Turn left at the road and soon branch right at a triangular green – where those not parking at the pub may have left their car. Passing Wareside Primary School – which will be to your left – go along this quiet lane for ¹/₃ mile to where it turns left. There is a weather-boarded pair of houses at this point.

② Keep forward from the houses along the track labelled as a bridleway. After passing a pond on the left you will arrive at another weather-boarded house on the right. If you reach Morley Hall Cottage you have gone too far! The point of departure from the track is along a right of way through the garden of the weather-boarded house. Surprising, but perfectly legal! For this go through the wide gate here and, passing a pond to your immediate left, soon make your exit through another gate.

③ On entering a field from the gate turn

Morley Ponds

right immediately, as directed by a waymark post. It's now a simple matter of following a sequence of two field edges, all the way to a road. The first field is accompanied by a hedge and, along part of its length, a long pond. The second field edge curves right then left and follows a ditch only.

④ Turn right at the road and, after about 120 yards, leave it for the *second* path on the left. This is marked as a 'Road used as a Public Path' and commences almost opposite the drive to Milletes New Hall. The path starts from a field corner and follows a hedge and ditch on the right. From the field corner at the far end turn right into a wide path between hedges, with a ditch on the right. When you meet a raised farm track at a T-junction turn right into it, and soon right again to pass Legges Cottage. Ignoring any branching paths, stay with the track all the way to a road – the one you left earlier!

⑤ Cross both the triangular green and the road to a kissing-gate opposite, where your destination – Wareside – is signposted. The route is now more or less straight on through a series of gates and four fields, with a raised path linking the second to the third field. At the far end of the fourth field the hedge on you right forms a corner and two ditches come together. Two footpaths fan out across the next field from this point and both lead ultimately to Wareside. We take the one going straight on to a footbridge in the far right-hand corner of the field – *not* the stile to the left of this.

⑥ From the footbridge turn left into the next field and follow its left-hand edge (maintaining your previous direction) to a pedestrian gate in the corner. Another gate immediately places you on a fenced path, and this in turn sees you back at the green by Wareside Primary School – where you may have left your car. If not, go left along the road and join the footpath on the right after 50 yards; then follow this down to the B1004 and the White Horse.

PLACES OF INTEREST NEARBY

Scott's Grotto in Ware consists of intriguing underground passages and chambers dug into the hillside and decorated with flints, shells and pebbles. It is open from April to end September every Saturday and Bank Holiday Monday from 2 pm to 4.30 pm. Telephone: 01920 464131.

Sawbridgeworth
The Old Bell

DIRECTIONS TO START: SAWBRIDGEWORTH LIES ON THE A1184 MIDWAY BETWEEN HARLOW AND BISHOP'S STORTFORD. THE OLD BELL IS IN BELL STREET, A ONE-WAY STREET ACCESSIBLE FROM THE A1184. THERE IS ALSO A FREQUENT RAIL SERVICE FROM LONDON (LIVERPOOL STREET). **PARKING:** IN THE PUB'S CAR PARK OR IN THE LARGE PUBLIC CAR PARK OFF BELL STREET – FREE AT WEEKENDS.

If you approach the town centre from the railway station and have an eye for the town's architecture, you will not be surprised to learn that Sawbridgeworth prospered from its malting and milling industries. The river Stort enhances the attractiveness and interest of the area as it passes between the town and the railway.

From Bell Street the walk takes the shortest route down to the river Stort, and includes St Mary's lovely churchyard. There follows 1½ miles of this unspoilt river – as far as the northern extremity of Harlow. You then double back along the opposite bank, soon striking 'inland' across fields to the fabulous Pishiobury estate, where the views and the fine estate trees are beyond compare.

The Old Bell

Among Sawbridgeworth's many remaining public houses, this is one of the oldest. In the heyday of stage coaches it was a favoured stop-off between Hertford and Harwich. Its popularity remains much in evidence today.

The lunchtime menu offers good traditional pub fare. Included is an exhaustive range of sandwiches; also burgers, salads, ploughman's, filled jacket potatoes and omelettes. The Old Bell brunch would certainly be worth a try, as would the intriguing choice of 'dippers'. Since lunches are not available on Sundays you could try one of the town's other pubs, in particular those in Knight Street, nearby.

Four real ales are always on offer at the Old Bell; also a range of wines by the glass. The pub keeps traditional opening hours, with no extended opening at weekends or during the summer. So you will need to time your walk carefully! Telephone: 01279 836003.

The Walk

① Turn right on leaving the Old Bell and cross The Square to Church Street. This will soon place you at the entrance to St Mary's churchyard. Passing immediately to the right of the church, follow the churchyard path downhill and continue forward between gardens. Stay on the path (a parallel road appears briefly on the left) and turn right with it at the bottom, soon turning left into a road. An imitation brewery complex (modern houses, no less!) comes into view on the left and the road eventually meets the river Stort.

② Leave the road by turning right onto

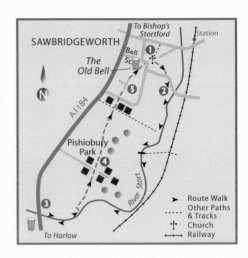

the towpath where it follows the right bank of the river. After ½ mile a footbridge takes you across to the opposite bank, where you should continue following the river. At the lock gate ahead go forward through a pedestrian gate and continue for another mile to the A1184 road – where the Harlow Mill Beefeater may stop you in your tracks!

③ Cross the road bridge to the opposite bank and double back alongside the river, firstly over a weir, then behind houses. After passing the houses go through a kissing-gate and enter a field, at its corner. Stay with the river for ¼ mile (measured from the A1184) as far as a distinct S-bend in its course. Where the river curves right out of the 'S' and where a wire fence bars further forward progress, turn left and follow the fence 'inland' to a field corner, where a stream flows nearby. Go through a kissing-gate on the right here and follow the course of the stream, which flows unseen under a line of trees about 10 yards to your left. After 100 yards or so go through a gap on the left into a field corner,

Fair Green at the end of the walk

where the stream runs briefly underground. Follow the field's right-hand edge (half-left to your previous direction), aiming for what appears to be the mid-point of a line of houses and passing three manhole covers on the way.

④ Pass briefly between gardens and cross a drive (beautifully lined with trees and lawns) to a kissing-gate opposite. On the right you have a view of a Pishiobury, a mansion built (or more correctly *rebuilt*) after a fire by James Wyatt in 1782. It is now occupied by a waste management company. On entering a field from the next kissing-gate, go forward along the right-hand edge and connect with a fine avenue of trees where the field corners meet. The parkland hereabouts was once part of the Pishiobury estate, its 'big house' being the one we viewed from the drive. With a magnificent green valley in view to your right, walk along the avenue to a kissing-gate at the far end. From there continue

forward along a path between gardens, soon crossing Brook Road to another path and keeping forward over the brook itself.

⑤ On joining a road at a cul-de-sac keep forward again, but now uphill through an attractive cottage settlement. Keep straight on beyond the cottages, on a tarmac path alongside a green and play area. You will shortly emerge at the attractive Fair Green (fair indeed!), with the church spire in view above the houses. Turn slightly left here for The Square, beyond which lies Bell Street and the Old Bell.

PLACES OF INTEREST NEARBY

The National Trust's **Hatfield Forest** lies 3 miles east of Bishop's Stortford, in Essex, and is signposted from the A120 at Takeley. Described as an 'outstanding ancient woodland' the forest is noted for its pollarded oaks and hornbeams and for its variety of wildlife. A charge is made for use of the car park.

Water End
The Red Lion

DIRECTIONS TO START: WATER END IS 2 MILES NORTH-WEST OF HEMEL HEMPSTEAD ON THE A4146. THE RED LION IS EASILY FOUND ALONGSIDE THIS ROAD. **PARKING:** THE PUB HAS ITS OWN CAR PARK. LIMITED ROADSIDE PARKING IS POSSIBLE IN THE POTTEN END ROAD NEARBY. ACCESS TO THIS (FROM HEMEL HEMPSTEAD) IS BY DRIVING OVER THE RIVER BRIDGE AND TURNING LEFT.

The lovely river Gade passes under the road near the Red Lion and again before flowing through meadows behind Water End's cottage settlement. A beautiful spot indeed, and overlooked from above by Gaddesden Place, an imposing Palladian villa.

While ascending the hillside (a long steady climb) opposite the Red Lion, the walk enjoys a magnificent panoramic view of the Gade valley. The view is retained as the walk traverses the hillside to Wood Farm. On returning to the valley floor it meets the peaceful village of Piccotts End and thereafter follows meadow and field edges back to Water End.

The Red Lion

The Red Lion continues its centuries-old tradition as a roadside inn but now as a well-known Chef and Brewer pub, open for as many hours as God provides – well, almost! You can drop in for a meal lunchtime to late evening any day and choose from a truly impressive menu. On the blackboard I counted no less than 34 main courses – including vegetarian dishes – and 14 starters! And if that isn't enough the snack menu lists sandwiches, filled jacket potatoes, ploughman's and 'hot hobs' (hot filled baguettes). Further blackboard menus include soups, sweets and children's choices, while in winter the 'game specials' board is likely to include such specialities as venison in red wine sauce or wild boar sausages. All this can be enjoyed in the comfort and atmosphere which is typical of these large food-orientated pubs. Drinkers should be equally happy with the selection of hand-pulled ales and the extensive wine list.

There are areas set aside for families and a garden for sun-worshippers in summer! Telephone: 01442 213594.

The Walk

① From the Red Lion cross the road (the A4146) to Red Lion Lane opposite. When the lane soon turns left go forward and uphill on a signposted bridleway, following a hedge (of sorts) on the left. Hemel Hempstead with its church steeple comes into view on the right and the bridleway eventually levels out. When the left-hand hedge terminates at a crossing and waymark post, keep straight on, with a hedge now on your right.

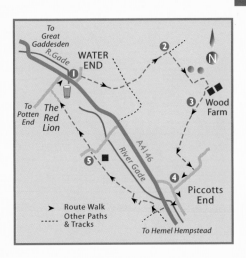

② Where overhead wires cross your route near the top of the hill, turn right from a waymark post through a hedge-gap and walk on the level path alongside a line of oak trees, which are in turn followed by a wood edge. Go over a stile in the far left-hand corner of the field and cross another field slightly left towards farm buildings (Wood Farm), aiming for a footpath signpost. Strictly speaking the right of way follows the left-hand field edge to the farm, although the waymark directs you across the field. Don't cross the stile by the farm but turn right and go downhill, soon following a hedge to a stile in the field's left-hand corner.

③ Continue straight on downhill in the next much larger field, following a hedge on the left to a gap in the far corner. Forward again, but now across a field and turning left into a farm track on arrival at the far side. The track and its accompanying hedge will deposit you on Dodds Lane where you can choose to turn right into the lane or into the adjacent field path running parallel to the lane. Either

The river Gade

route will take you down to the road at Piccotts End.

④ Turn left at the road and soon find yourself beside the magnificent Old Mill House. The mill and the mill house were for some time in a sad state of dereliction, but, as you can see, there has been a remarkable transformation into very desirable dwellings. Although your next move is to turn into the drive alongside the Old Mill House you may care to continue in the road for a short distance to a terrace of timber-framed houses set back from the road. It was in one of these houses that a number of 15th century wall paintings were discovered in 1953.

Back at the drive by the Old Mill House, soon cross the river Gade to the busy A4146. Go straight over this to a gate and drive by the Three Valleys Water pumping station. Walk along the drive almost as far as the next gate (there

is a house beyond it) and pass through a kissing-gate on the right. Initially continuing in your previous direction, you should rotate clockwise around three sides of an enclosed area, with a metal fence on the right all the way. A kissing-gate will then set you on course parallel to the valley. The path meanders widely between the trees and a meadow before running more or less straight on along the lower edge of an arable field. Cross a stile in the far right-hand corner of this long field and keep forward along another (well mown) field to another stile, passing Gaddesden Hall en route.

⑤ Continuing forward through another, smaller field, leave this from its far right-hand corner and step onto a drive. With Gaddesden Hall now behind you, leave the drive immediately (it turns left here) by going forward on a narrow path. When you soon enter the fields keep straight on along the right-hand edge, passing a clump of tall trees as you go. Leave the second field at a stile and gate 50 yards before the far right-hand corner and resume your former direction, but now along a rough drive by the houses. Turning right along the road at the end (Potten End Hill) you might have a view of Gaddesden Place on the hilltop ahead. Another right turn – into the A4146 – will soon lead you over the river Gade to the Red Lion pub.

PLACES OF INTEREST NEARBY

Gradebridge Park is a delightful public open space two miles south of Water End. For this take the A4146 in the Hemel Hempstead direction and turn first left for Picotts End. Continuing straight on you will find the Park on your right, and beyond that the lovely Hemel Hempstead Old Town, with its fine houses, shops and eating places.

Northchurch
The George and Dragon

MAP: OS EXPLORER 181 (GR 974088)   **WALK 23**   **DISTANCE:** 3¾ MILES

DIRECTIONS TO START: NORTHCHURCH IS ONE MILE NORTH-WEST OF BERKHAMSTED ALONG THE A4251 (PREVIOUSLY THE A41). THE GEORGE AND DRAGON IS SITUATED ON THIS ROAD OPPOSITE THE PARISH CHURCH. **PARKING:** IN THE PUB'S LARGE CAR PARK OR IN NEW ROAD, A SHORT DISTANCE INTO THE WALK. A CONVENIENT ALTERNATIVE IS MANDELYNS, A SIDE ROAD OFF THE A4251 IN THE TRING DIRECTION.

Although Northchurch appears as a suburb of Berkhamsted, it retains some of its earlier character as a village on the old London Road. Now that the A41 traffic has moved away, Northchurch can put the clock back just a little. The nearby Grand Union Canal is a reminder of those earlier days, while the railway places the locality well within the 21st century.

The walk follows the towpath of the canal to Dudswell and Cow Roast. From Cow Roast it crosses the old London Road and heads gently uphill towards (but not meeting) the new road – the A41. Exceptional views across the Bulbourne valley are enjoyed as the walk crosses arable fields on its way back to Dudswell and the canal. The walk concludes by retracing the canal towpath back to Northchurch.

The George and Dragon

Those who know Northchurch as just a place to drive through are missing one of Hertfordshire's gems. It's called the George and Dragon! With its comfortable dining and drinking areas, old oak beams and real open fire, it strikes a very nice balance between a 'locals' pub' and a pub where visitors can enjoy a drink and a good meal in an old-world atmosphere.

Lunches are served from Monday to Saturday only (12 noon to 2 pm). In the main it's all traditional English food. Sandwiches and ploughman's are available, and there is a daily specials board. If the absence of food on a Sunday is a problem, you could call instead at the Cow Roast Inn halfway along the walk. A roast lunch and a selection of main meals is available there on Sundays until 5 pm. You could of course start the walk there (point 3).

The landlord of the George and Dragon confesses to having a 'pretty good range of beers' from his four handpumps. An alternative to beer would be one of the small selection of wines. Children are welcome if having meals. Telephone: 01442 864533.

The Walk

① Go left along the road from the George and Dragon and turn right into New Road, by the school playground. After crossing the river Bulbourne turn left to join the canal towpath. There's little to be said as you walk the first ¾ mile of towpath to the road at Dudswell Lock, except 'enjoy it', as I did! On arrival at the lock, cross the road bridge to the towpath on the opposite bank.

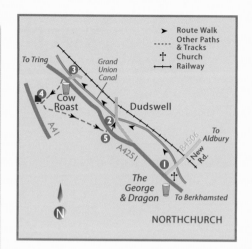

② From Dudswell there's a slightly shorter stretch of canal (⅔ mile) to Cow Roast Lock (at road bridge no. 137). You are on the summit level of the canal hereabouts, which explains the '1946' brick-built pumping station near the lock cottage at Cow Roast. In order to maintain a sufficient level it is necessary to pump water up from the chalk aquifers which lie underground.

③ Leave the canal here and go left along the lane to the A4251, crossing this to the Cow Roast Inn opposite. The site of the inn was a regular stopping-off point for cattle drovers on their way to London. It has been said that the drovers would reduce their charges by one animal just here, roasting it on the spot! Join the bridleway (signposted 'Chiltern Way') which commences to the right of the inn and follow it straight on and gradually uphill until, after ¼ mile, you detect a distinct S-bend in its route. This is about 200 yards before the A41 road.

④ Leave the bridleway just before the S-

Dudswell Lock

bend and, after passing under trees, enter a sports field and walk along its upper edge. Go over a stile in the far right-hand corner of the sports field and keep forward, gradually climbing the hill along the edge of the left-hand field. The view opens up as you approach the summit – Northchurch ahead, Aldbury and Northchurch Commons over to your left. When the hedge on your right terminates, keep forward (more correctly quarter left!) alongside a fence aiming for the far left-hand corner. A kissing-gate down there will place you on the A4251 once again.

⑤ Go forward on the road for 50 yards then cross to a short path and the closed end of Boswick Lane. Follow the lane straight on to a T-junction and turn left for the canal. After joining the towpath to the right of the bridge (a right-hand turn from the lane), retrace your steps back to the next bridge, which is numbered 139. Turn right at the road there and you will soon be back at the George and Dragon.

PLACES OF INTEREST NEARBY

The National Trust woodlands of **Aldbury and Ivinghoe Commons** can be enjoyed by driving north along the B4506 from Northchurch (starting from New Road). For the lovely village of Aldbury turn first left after 2 miles; for the National Trust Visitor Centre and tearoom take the next left turn after a further ⅔ mile. The tearoom is open January to early December from 12 noon to 5 pm, Tuesday to Sunday. Telephone: 01442 851227.

Potten End
The Plough

DIRECTIONS TO START: POTTEN END IS SIGNPOSTED FROM WATER END ON THE A4146, 3 MILES NORTH-WEST OF HEMEL HEMPSTEAD. ON ARRIVAL AT POTTEN END, TURN RIGHT INTO THE FRONT AND, FOR THE PLOUGH, RIGHT AGAIN INTO PLOUGH LANE. **PARKING:** THE PUB DOES NOT HAVE ITS OWN CAR PARK. THERE IS ROADSIDE PARKING NEARBY.

This lovely village of Potten End, with its green, its cottages and its cottage gardens, complements the countryside around. Nearby are the woodland outposts of the great Ashridge estate, while a little to the north lies Frithsden in its peaceful valley.

Commencing along The Front, arguably Potten End's most attractive street, the walk soon enters the Old Green, an idyllic open space behind the houses. It enjoys a magnificent view across Frithsden's valley, where lies the Alford Arms and Frithsden Vineyard. A steady climb takes the walk up through Little Frithsden Copse; and a further stretch places it on The Green at Potten End.

The Plough

This is a good example of a genuine country pub that offers the best in atmosphere and creature comforts. Situated in a quiet road it overlooks one of Potten End's greens. A comprehensive menu is available at lunchtimes and evenings except Sunday evening. This includes soup, toasties, 'jaw busters' (French bread served with various fillings), meat and vegetarian burgers, salads, ploughman's and filled jacket potatoes. The specials board might typically include steak and kidney pudding, rump steak, and an 'all day breakfast'. On Sunday the lunch consists of a good value roast in addition to bar food and a special Thai menu. You are well advised to book this in advance. As pointed out in a footnote on the specials board 'all fresh meat and vegetables are supplied by a local farm shop'. A children's menu is available – so children are obviously welcome here! Walking and cycling groups are also very welcome.

Four real ales are offered; also a selection of lagers and wines. The pub is open 'all day, every day'. Telephone: 01442 865391.

The Walk

① Go left along the road from the Plough and turn left at the crossing into The Front, an intriguing street name, you will agree! Join a footpath on the left just beyond the last house – almost at the road junction – and soon find yourself on the Old Green, a lovely open area which was 'given to the village in 1977'. A plaque to that effect makes its appearance, as does a large log-hewn seat, from which point you should

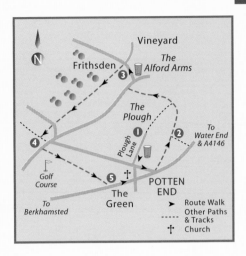

keep to the upper, most used, of two paths, while ignoring a lesser branch on the right quite soon.

② When a signposted path comes in from the right, keep forward on what becomes a tree-shaded bridleway, with fields on each side. In due course a path comes in from the left (for information only!) and a magnificent view opens up on the right – the Frithsden valley in all it glory! On meeting a road at the bottom, turn right; then turn left at the first junction. You will soon have the welcoming sight of the Alford Arms, a well-placed halfway house! Apart from the pub, there are two worthwhile diversions from this point: a right turn to Frithsden Vineyard (see Places of Interest) and straight on along the road for a more complete view of Frithsden.

③ Back at the Alford Arms, cross the road to the bridleway opposite and climb the slope under trees, with a field in view to the left. On meeting a quiet road after ³/₄ mile (this serves an estate of neatly-placed

Frithsden

houses and gardens) cross to a hedge-lined path opposite. The path runs between gardens and emerges into woodland. Keeping forward through the wood, very soon meet a bridleway at a T-junction. Turn left here (into the 'Hertfordshire Way') and join a road.

④ You should normally turn right in the road and leave it after 30 yards for a sunken bridleway under trees on the left, but since this may well be muddy you could cross the road directly to an alternative path opposite. After crossing a golf course (the two routes converge here) you should continue forward under the trees, either along the bridleway or along another alternative path running parallel on the left. You will eventually come in sight of houses and will closely follow their gardens. Ignoring a branch on the left – which passes between the houses – continue alongside the gardens and veer right to a road.

⑤ Directly opposite is (or should be!) The Green at Potten End. You could cross this to the village pond and take your ease at the nearby seat; or you could simply turn left along the road and, for the Plough, left into Church Road.

PLACES OF INTEREST NEARBY

Frithsden Vineyard is close to the halfway point of the walk. It is usually open to the public on Wednesday to Sunday from 10 am to 5 pm. There are wine tastings and sales, and you can walk around the vineyard. Please phone beforehand if you intend to visit: 01442 864732. **Berkhamsted Castle** ruin is also open to the public daily. It is here (when there was an earlier building) that William the Conqueror received the submission of the Saxon leaders after the Battle of Hastings.

Brickendon
The Farmer's Boy

MAP: OS EXPLORER 174 (GR 323081)   **WALK 25**   **DISTANCE:** 3½ MILES

DIRECTIONS TO START: IF COMING FROM THE A414 AT HERTFORD, JOIN THE B158 ON THE SOUTH SIDE OF THE TOWN (ESSENDON DIRECTION) AND, PASSING COUNTY HALL, TURN LEFT INTO BRICKENDON LANE JUST BEYOND THE RAILWAY BRIDGE. BRICKENDON IS 2½ MILES ALONG THIS ROAD. **PARKING:** IN THE PUB'S CAR PARK ACROSS THE ROAD OR ALONG THE ROADSIDE NEARBY.

Brickendon is close to a vast expanse of woodland comprising at least eight named areas, but known collectively as Broxbourne Woods. With their abundance of rides and footpaths the woods offer endless possibilities for walkers and for those interested in woodland management and wildlife.

On this walk we explore just one part of Broxbourne Woods – in the area bounded by Highfield and Cowheath Woods. We tread wide, hopefully sunlit, drives and woodland paths, crossed or accompanied here and there by watercourses. We pass Dane Mead nature reserve, with its opportunity for a short diversion, and perhaps see a muntjac deer or hear a woodpecker drumming.

The Farmer's Boy

The Farmer's Boy is just about all that anyone could desire from a village pub. It has comfort and a welcoming atmosphere; it is open 'all day, every day'; and it offers meals and snacks throughout the day. So if you are delayed on the walk, no matter! The 'all day lunch menu', available in the bar, runs from 11 am to 9.30 pm and includes an impressive choice of dishes, all at the same price. The snack menu in the bar runs from 11 am to 3 pm and offers oven baked potatoes, ploughman's, omelettes and baguettes. The restaurant menu is even more impressive – with about 30 dishes on the first count! You will need to book ahead for Sunday lunch unless you just want a snack.

Four to five real ales are provided, and a similar number of lagers. Well-behaved children are welcome in the restaurant. In summer the spectacle and aroma of a spit roast or barbecue might attract you out into the garden. Telephone: 01992 511610.

The Walk

① You could, if you wish, drive the first part of the walk from the pub. This will relieve you of ¼ mile of road walking (a fairly quiet road as it happens) at the start and finish of the walk.

On leaving the pub go left along the road in the Hertford direction and, after passing a pond on the left, join a drive (Bourne Orchard) leaving from the right. If you arrived at this point by car you could park on the grass here or further along the road.

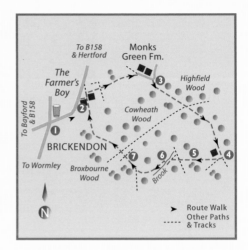

② Along the drive you will pass Wellpond Cottage. On reaching the large house at the end of the drive you should turn left and go through a kissing-gate into a field corner, with the pond now behind you. Keep to the right-hand edge of the field initially, then cross it straight on to another gate by an electricity pole (you will notice that the field is L-shaped). Go over a farm track from the gate and continue forward in the next field, aiming for the right-hand extremity of a long narrow wood and following a short hedge to a corner. Cross a footbridge in this left-hand corner and turn right through a kissing-gate into the adjacent field and follow its right-hand edge; then make your way to a pair of gates placed centrally at the far end of the next field. From the gates a rough drive takes you forward to Monks Green Farm. The surface changes to tarmac and the drive turns left beyond the buildings, which is where you should leave it.

③ From the gate on the right go along a bridleway and turn left with it after 120 yards. You are now in Highfield Wood,

Highfield Wood

narrow path waymarked with arrows. The wider bridleway keeps to the left from this point – but that's for information only! Taking guidance from the arrows and staying within 20–30 yards of the denser part of the wood on the left, you should eventually reach a stile in a timber and wire fence at the far end. If you fail to find the stile it will be necessary to follow the fence uphill until you do!

⑤ After crossing the stile turn left, then right into a path after a few yards to resume your previous direction. Keeping forward on this good clear path you will eventually go over a crossing and soon join forces with a track coming in from the right. Going half-left into this you will, after 65 yards, arrive at a stile. Keep forward here, into the open and with a gully running parallel on the right, all the way to a footbridge at the bottom.

⑥ After crossing the footbridge go uphill on the clear path and turn left at a T-junction near the top after 50 yards. You will again be parallel with the gully – at least to start with – but on its right-hand side, while still following the arrows. Ignoring a branch coming in from the left and keeping forward over a crossing, you will eventually have the welcome sight of a seat.

⑦ Keep forward from the seat, turning left a little very soon and crossing a wide drive after 50 yards (measured from the seat), eventually meeting the fields beyond a pedestrian gate. Go straight on along the two ensuing field edges, passing a pond in the first field and emerging onto a wide grassy path. Turn left into the drive at the far end – by the large house met near the start of the walk – and left again at the road. It's now a ¼ mile back to the Farmer's Boy.

where a marvellous track takes you straight on and gradually downhill, then over a crossing-track and more steeply down to a brook at the bottom, where a board announces Dane Mead nature reserve. Pastures come into view on the right as you climb out of the dip, as does the house called Brambles Wood, also on the right.

④ You will soon (90 yards from the house) find yourself beside a waymark post and, 30 yards further on, an information board explaining the history and wildlife of the area. This is the point at which you should leave the track, and where you should take more care than usual! A footpath and a bridleway are waymarked as leaving the track here, each in a separate direction. We need to be sure to take the footpath, which is in fact due west. Take care because there are three or so routes leaving from the right. When confronted by four massive (and magnificent!) oak trees after only 80 yards you should bear a little to the right into a

Goose Green
The Huntsman

MAP: OS EXPLORER 174 (GR 353090)　　**WALK 26**　　DISTANCE: 2 MILES

DIRECTIONS TO START: TAKE THE HODDESDON TURN-OFF FROM THE A10 AND TURN RIGHT AT THE FIRST ROUNDABOUT. TURN FIRST RIGHT INTO PAUL'S LANE – WHICH BECOMES TAVENORS LANE – THEN FIRST RIGHT INTO LORD STREET FOR THE 1½ MILE DRIVE TO GOOSE GREEN. **PARKING:** THERE IS AMPLE SPACE IN THE PUB'S CAR PARK. ROADSIDE PARKING IS POSSIBLE BUT NOT IDEAL.

Today we stay entirely within the confines of the Woodland Trust's Hoddesdon Park Wood, which forms part of a vast complex of woodlands extending south-west from Hoddesdon. It is heralded as containing 'one of the best examples of sessile oak and hornbeam woodland in the county'. More than that it is simply a lovely wood in which to walk!

Using the central north-south drive (a wide track) the walk makes for the southern extremity of the wood. It turns west to follow the meandering Spital Brook, where there are lovely meadows in view beyond the opposite bank. It comes within sight of the Roman road, Ermine Street, before turning yet again and following waymarked paths back to Goose Green.

The Huntsman

There must be few pubs in a more unique and attractive setting than the Huntsman. Tucked away off a quiet road between Box Wood and Hoddesdon Park Wood, yet minutes away from a busy town, it is well recognised as a venue for walking and cycling groups who come here for a good meal and a drink to enhance their outing. Those requiring a light lunch choose from the daily bar menu of ploughman's and garnished sandwiches – 'all served with that extra-special smile'! For a more substantial meal, or in the evenings, the blackboard menu is consulted. This changes daily and is likely to include dishes such as braised shoulder of lamb, Chicken Italian, and broccoli and Stilton quiche. In addition to chicken or lamb, a sumptuous 'whole half beef strip loin' is roasted on Sunday. There is also a choice of traditional main meals at that time, including a vegetarian dish. And there is more – in the form of an irresistible selection of desserts!

Families are very welcome here. In summer the children may want to be outside – chatting to the goats, chickens and rabbits!

The pub is open at the traditional hours from Monday to Thursday, but 'all day' from Friday to Sunday. Meals are available lunchtimes and evenings, but continuously from 12 noon to 7 pm on Sundays. Telephone: 01992 443294.

The Walk

① Turn right along the road from the Huntsman and go through a gate on the left after 100 yards, opposite Woodcock Cottage. This leads into Hoddesdon Park

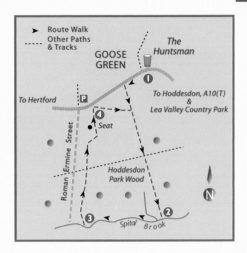

Wood. Although there are statutory rights of way in the wood, we largely make use of permissive paths and tracks. The rights of way are marked with yellow arrows (for footpaths) while the permissive paths are often marked with striped posts or National Nature Reserve green arrows. The first part of our walk is straight on along the main drive (a wide track), ignoring all branches and crossings until arriving at the far end of the wood. That's more than ½ mile of the walk completed already!

② Turn right at the far end of the wood and follow the meandering Spital Brook, soon crossing a tributary (which may be dry) and walking alongside the brook all the way to a pedestrian gate. That's another ¼ mile or so. Without going through the gate you will see a meeting of ways ahead, also two footbridges and an entrance to a nature reserve of the Herts and Middlesex Wildlife Trust. The main track running left to right is Ermine Street, built by the Romans to connect London to York.

③ Now you should retrace your steps back

View across the Spital Brook

from the gate – with the brook then on your right – and join a path on the left after about 50 yards, just beyond a small footbridge. The path is labelled with a waymark and runs uphill from the brook. Had you not walked as far as the gate this path would have required a half-right turn. Go straight over a skewed crossing-path very soon and commence a long steady ascent through the wood, guided by the waymarks. You will cross a wide track – with a gate in view 50 yards to the left – and eventually have sight of a field and a gully about 100 yards ahead. Continuing with the waymarks (and while that field is still 100 yards ahead) go half-right, downhill, then over a footbridge after 50 yards. It's uphill now eventually turning left and passing a seat. Then it's back to, but not entering, the road – unless you have a liking for tarmac!

④ With your back to the road, follow the main footpath downhill to a footbridge; then uphill (ignoring a left-hand branch) and back to the central drive where the walk started. Turn left there and right at the road for the Huntsman.

PLACES OF INTEREST NEARBY

Lea Valley Country Park follows the course of the river Lea and the Lea Navigation (a canal) from Ware to Stratford. A vast range of recreational facilities and outdoor interests are catered for. Among the nearest to Goose Green is the 15th century **Rye House**, a moated gatehouse close to Rye House station, Hoddesdon. It is open at weekends and bank holidays from Easter to the end of September 11am to 5pm. Telephone: 01992 702200.

Tyttenhanger
The Plough

MAP: OS EXPLORER 182 (GR 183059)   **WALK 27**   **DISTANCE:** 2 MILES

DIRECTIONS TO START: TYTTENHANGER VILLAGE AND THE PLOUGH ARE ALONG A QUIET COUNTRY LANE ½ MILE NORTH-WEST OF THE A414 BETWEEN LONDON COLNEY AND HATFIELD. FROM LONDON COLNEY ROUNDABOUT (JUNCTION OF A414 AND A1081) DRIVE ALONG THE A414 IN THE HATFIELD DIRECTION AND TURN LEFT AFTER ½ MILE INTO HIGHFIELD LANE; THEN, FOR THE PLOUGH, TURN FIRST RIGHT INTO TYTTENHANGER GREEN. RETURNING TO THE ROUNDABOUT IS MORE DIFFICULT (LEFT ONLY AT THE A414) AND IT WOULD BE BETTER TO GO RIGHT ON LEAVING THE PLOUGH AND TURN SECOND RIGHT FOR THE A414. **PARKING:** IN THE PUB'S CAR PARK OR ALONG THE ROADSIDE NEARBY.

It is gratifying to know that the sombre hospitals that inhabited this part of Hertfordshire have all closed and have been, or are being, transformed into pleasant community areas. One such is Hill End Hospital which we visit on this walk. Now in the care of Highfield Park Trust, it is an interesting and attractive locality to explore.

In addition to field paths, the walk uses Hixberry Lane (a wide track) in its entirety. Since there are no hills to speak of – just one very moderate incline – this is an undemanding walk.

The Plough

In a quiet retreat away from busy roads, the Plough is a magnet for those who know a good pub when they see one. Come 12 noon and they are there, ready to enjoy the good food and good ale for which the pub is renowned. Food is offered daily at lunchtimes – but not evenings – from a menu that should satisfy all tastes and constitutions. Sandwiches appear in their traditional form or with bloomer bread. Included are toasted sandwiches, 'BLTs' and Mike's Super Sarnie (Mike is the landlord!). If you enjoy kebabs, there are around 10 varieties to choose from. There is a similar range of burgers, salads and omelettes as well as a selection of vegetarian and fish dishes. If for once in your life you will throw health considerations to the wind, you could opt for one of the Plough's 'Guaranteed high-cholesterol fry-ups'! Go one step further and choose a delicious sweet from among those listed on the specials board.

The Plough offers no less than eight real ales at any one time and has been featured in the *Good Beer Guide* over many years. It is open daily at the traditional 'old-fashioned' hours.

The pub has a family room; also a conservatory for those who wish to eat in the light of day. In winter you may prefer the inner sanctum where there are no less than two real open fires. While in there you could take stock of the landlord's collection of 1,500 beer bottles which festoon the bar. Telephone: 01727 857777.

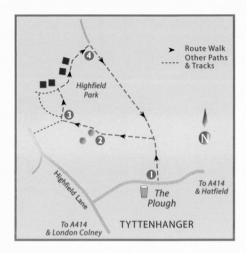

The Walk

① Turn right on leaving the Plough and go as far as a small pear-shaped triangular green – where the buses turn. Leave the road here and enter Hixberry Lane, a track on the left. Follow the track for less than ¼ mile to where it runs into a shallow dip. As you pull out of the dip a waymark post is your signal to leave the track (you will return to it later) for a footpath on the left. This runs along the edge of a field, with a ditch on the left. Soon enter the next, larger, field and cross this half-right (diagonally) to the right-hand extremity of a distant wood – beyond the summit of the field. If you pass a manhole cover in the process, you are on course!

② On reaching the field's far corner, you should briefly follow a track along the near wood edge, then continue in the same direction as previously, crossing the next field diagonally, corner to corner. Although a waymark in the final corner indicates a left turn into a sports field, you should go half-right through a gap, entering the grounds of Highfield Park Trust. The Trust was established after Hill End Hospital

Highfield Park

was closed to patients. A comprehensive range of facilities was planned for the park, including footpaths and cycleways, new woodland planting and a tree trail, renovation of an old apple orchard, restoration of sports areas, and much more.

③ You will, after 50 yards or so, pass through a gap in a row of tall trees. Turn right here and follow a path as it curves round to the left alongside trees and a hedge. Looking straight ahead you should see (trees permitting!) the dividing line between the original hospital buildings and an estate of new houses. You will go over a crossing-path before arriving at a tarmac drive close to those houses. Turn right into the drive and stay with it to its end, enjoying as you go the fine prospect of tall trees – with its tree trail – and the beautifully restored orchard. Enjoy also,

should you feel the need, one of the many seats that have been provided!

④ Leaving the park just beyond the orchard, turn right into a road, Hixberry Lane once more. As the lane soon evolves into a wide track you are on course for Tyttenhanger. Simply walk straight on for ²/₃ mile and turn right for the Plough at the far end.

PLACES OF INTEREST NEARBY

Bowmans Open Farm near London Colney is a working farm with a difference. Children's activities and a shop and refectory are provided along with a farm trail and demonstrations of animal husbandry. From Tyttenhanger and the A414 take the first exit – the A1081 – at the London Colney Roundabout, followed by the first exit at the next roundabout. Telephone: 01727 822106.

Epping Green
The Beehive

MAP: OS EXPLORER 182 (GR 296069)   **WALK 28**   **DISTANCE:** 2¼ MILES

DIRECTIONS TO START: FROM THE A414 EAST OF HATFIELD JOIN THE B1455 AND SOON TURN LEFT INTO THE B158. TURN FIRST RIGHT FROM THE B158, THEN LEFT BY THE CHURCH AND WAR MEMORIAL AT LITTLE BERKHAMSTED. EPPING GREEN IS ONE MILE ALONG THIS ROAD. THE B158 IS ALSO ACCESSIBLE FROM HERTFORD.
PARKING: IN THE PUB'S CAR PARK. ROADSIDE PARKING IS NOT ADVISED. YOU COULD ALTERNATIVELY START THE WALK AT LITTLE BERKHAMSTED (POINT 4), WHERE ROADSIDE PARKING IS EASIER.

There is something very special about this part of Hertfordshire. Perhaps it's the attractive villages – Little Berkhamsted, Essendon, Bayford – or perhaps it's the undulating landscape, its views and its snatches of woodland. What it all adds up to however is a most pleasant area in which to walk, and to return to again and again.

We take a sample of this by walking from Epping Green to Little Berkhamsted and back: firstly through fields to the lovely Buck's Alley Wood; then a stop at Little Berkhamsted to admire the church and its fine houses; penultimately along fieldside paths that offer some of the county's finest views.

The Beehive

My first clue as to the popularity of this pub was in the speed with which its large car park filled to capacity soon after midday on a Friday! Doubtless the pub's speciality – fresh fish – is the main attraction. This comes in dishes with cod, skate, plaice, swordfish, monkfish, haddock, king prawns... and more besides. Those not into fish could choose from an impressive selection of sandwiches, filled jacket potatoes, ploughman's or 'main courses'. Examples from the latter are steak and kidney suet pudding, lasagne, broccoli and cheese bake, vegetable curry and chicken in oyster sauce. On Sundays a full menu is offered, along with a traditional roast. There is an impressive choice of desserts, also a children's menu and smaller portions of certain dishes. Meals are available every lunchtime and evening from Monday to Saturday. Sunday lunch extends to 4 pm.

Two ales are available. These are Greene King IPA and Adnam's Bitter.

The pub is open at the traditional hours, except on Sunday when it closes around 5 pm. Telephone: 01707 875959.

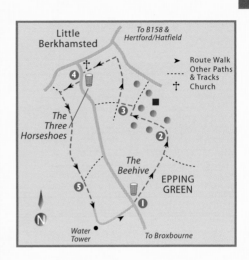

The Walk

① Turn left into the road from the pub's car park and immediately left through a gap. After following the field's left-hand border (a rough drive runs in parallel on the right) you should cross a farm track just beyond the field corner. Go straight on along the next two fields, mostly away from the left-hand edge and joining a track at the far end, at a bend. Go forward on this well-drained track under the trees and stay with it when it eventually curves left and evolves into something more like a path.

② A deep gully appears on the left and a footbridge takes you across it. The path then leads you into the undulating slopes of Buck's Alley Wood. After a brief ascent the path drops down to another gully then rises again and soon turns right. After about 100 yards from the turning you should leave the path for a stile a few yards uphill on the left. This should not be confused with an earlier unmarked path – which does not lead to a stile. Entering the field there go up to, *but not over*, a stile on the far side which leads to another, upper, field corner.

③ Without crossing that stile turn right to a kissing-gate and re-enter the wood. You will see a deep slope down to your right before entering another field. Ahead is Stratton's Folly – viewed in winter only, when the trees are bare! Built in 1789 this tower is said to have functioned as a terrestrial observatory for viewing shipping on the river Thames. Tell me another! Walking in that direction and following the

Buck's Alley Wood

overhead wires, enter the next field and go as far as a garden hedge near the field corner; then turn left and follow this and the next field edge straight on to Little Berkhamsted, by the churchyard of St Andrew's.

④ Notice the lovely terrace of cottages opposite the church before turning left along the road. Then after passing the Three Horseshoes pub go into the recreation field opposite the village hall, and leave it through a kissing-gate in the far right-hand corner. Turn left from the gate into a field and discover why I have brought you here – for that marvellous view westward! There is more of the same as you walk the next left-hand field edge and when you enter a track directly ahead.

⑤ Keep forward when another track comes in over your left shoulder, and again when the surface changes to tarmac. You will pass what was formerly Epping House School, which is a Grade II Listed Georgian mansion. And when the drive (for that's what it now is) turns left by a massive water tower, stay with it and eventually join the road at Epping Green – opposite the Beehive.

PLACES OF INTEREST NEARBY

Paradise Wildlife Park is in White Stubbs Lane in the Broxbourne direction and can be visited by turning left out of the Beehive. Follow this with a first left and, after that, a first right turn. The park is a popular attraction for families. Telephone: 01992 468001.

Colney Street
Moor Mill

MAP: OS EXPLORER 182 (GR 150024)   **WALK 29**   **DISTANCE:** 3 MILES

DIRECTIONS TO START: MOOR MILL IS 1½ MILES NORTH OF RADLETT AND IS EASILY FOUND JUST OFF THE A5183. JOIN SMUG OAK LANE IMMEDIATELY SOUTH OF THE M25 MOTORWAY CROSSING (NO ACCESS FROM THE M25 HERE) AND SOON TURN RIGHT FOR MOOR MILL. **PARKING:** MOOR MILL HAS A VERY LARGE CAR PARK. THERE IS ALSO THE RIVERSIDE WAY CAR PARK (NB: CLOSES AT DUSK) OFF DROP LANE A SHORT DISTANCE INTO THE WALK. ROADSIDE PARKING IS LIMITED.

A glance at the map of this part of Hertfordshire might lead you to think that there has been a takeover by motorways, trunk roads and railways. However, the presence of the rivers Colne and Ver – which converge here – ensures that there is still much unspoilt countryside to explore. There are lovely views and a profusion of wildlife to enjoy – perhaps even a kingfisher or two!

The walk commences by following the ¾ mile long Riverside Way which runs alongside the river Ver. Where the Ver meets the Colne the walk doubles back, in sight of the Colne now, and with a glimpse of the magnificent Netherwylde farmhouse.

Moor Mill

The close proximity of Moor Mill to the M25 motorway is fully compensated for by the historical interest and fascination of this inn. It retains much of the original apparatus and machinery from the watermill of 1762, including two massive waterwheels, one of which still turns. A mill has stood on this site for more than 1,000 years – as far back as Saxon times. The mill's function has changed, but its historical perspective is retained and honoured.

If you dine in one of the eating areas on the first or second floor of the mill, you can enjoy from the upper floor, a view of the mill stream (the river Ver), and its pond. On a warm summer's day you could be out there yourself, making use of one of the many picnic tables – consuming pub food or drink of course! Families will be well pleased with the facilities on offer, including a safe play area.

Whether you contemplate a snack or a main meal you should find your needs well satisfied with the regular menu or the specials board. The former includes filled jacket potatoes, freshly baked baguettes with hot or cold fillings, and a wide choice of main meals. The excellent children's menu conveys the respect that the 'smaller guests' deserve, with its choice of two-course (or three) meals and its complete absence of fish fingers and chicken nuggets!

Two real ales are available. Flower's Original and Wadworth 6X.

Moor Mill is open 'all day, every day', with food available from 12 noon until late in the day. Telephone: 01727 875557.

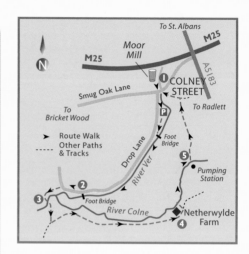

The Walk

① On leaving Moor Mill's entrance drive, cross over Smug Oak Lane to the right-hand of the two bridleways opposite. This runs to the right of the river Ver and is waymarked as the Ver Valley Walk. You will soon cross a concrete drive before walking parallel to Drop Lane. After passing to the left of Drop Lane car park and going forward between fences, you will cross a bridge to the left-hand side of the river. If starting from the car park you will need to turn right into that path.

② After a further ¾ mile the path re-crosses the river and connects with Drop Lane. This is where the Riverside Way terminates. Turn left into the lane and stay with it for 150 yards to where it turns right. Had you been on a horse you could have shortened the trot a little by taking the bridleway option here and crossing the ford to your left! Assuming you are on foot go through the kissing-gate ahead and follow the right bank of the river along a field edge. It is along here that the rivers Colne

The river Colne

you to the south of an extensive pumping station before passing the entrance to residential Dutch Barn. The right-hand branch 50 yards before Dutch Barn should be ignored

④ At a junction of ways ahead an opening on the left reveals the façade of the attractive Netherwylde farmhouse. Keeping forward here (for 'Watling Street') you will soon be joined by a drive coming in over your left shoulder. A few paces more and you should leave the bridleway for a signposted hedge-gap on the left. After crossing the river turn right immediately and cross an extensive area of scrub and grass to a footbridge. This will place you in the sharp corner of a very large field. Go along the right-hand field edge – with the river Colne over to your right – and eventually arrive near a well-disguised pumping station.

⑤ Turn left now and, following a ditch on your right, walk between fields to a farm track at the far end. Go left along the track and soon arrive back at Smug Oak Lane and Moor Mill.

and Ver join forces, the Colne having come down from Colney Heath and London Colney.

③ Go over the footbridge to the field opposite (prior to overhead wires) and follow the curving path to a stile on the far side. Take care not to go charging on, but turn very sharp left into a bridleway, more correctly a RUPP – a 'Road used as a Public Path'. Anything less like a road could hardly be imagined! The bridleway elevates

> **PLACES OF INTEREST NEARBY**
> **St Albans City**, 3 miles north along the A5183 has a wealth of interest including the Abbey (and its excellent refectory!), Verulamium Park and Museum, and the Roman Amphitheatre. St Albans was an important town in the Roman Empire.

Belsize
The Plough

MAP: OS EXPLORER 182 (GR 034009) · **WALK 30** · **DISTANCE:** 1¾ MILES

DIRECTIONS TO START: FROM KINGS LANGLEY'S HIGH STREET (THE A4251) JOIN THE UPHILL VICARAGE LANE AND DRIVE ABSOLUTELY STRAIGHT ON FOR 2½ MILES TO BELSIZE. KINGS LANGLEY IS 1 MILE FROM JUNCTION 20 OF THE M25. **PARKING:** IN THE PUB'S CAR PARK OR ALONG THE ROADSIDE NEARBY.

Cradled in a crossing of country ways, the little hamlet of Belsize is one of Hertfordshire's contributions to the attractive Chiltern scene, albeit many miles from its well-known escarpment. Being modestly profiled the hills and valleys hereabouts provide the walker with numerous pleasurable and undemanding possibilities.

On leaving the Plough the walk soon meets the now wooded site of Penman's Green where, in times past, sheep were *penned*, rested and watered on their way to market. Trees, wildflowers, birds, mammals, and insects – and public enjoyment – now have prior claim on this piece of woodland. Beyond the Green the walk crosses grazing land and enjoys a lovely woodland of beech, chestnut and holly followed by an impressive cross-field view of Belsize.

The Plough

Passers-by who take delight in the outward appearance of the Plough would not fail to be disappointed should they chance to go inside. This is a real village pub where the tenants tenaciously hold to traditional values while offering the best in creature comforts. In winter there is the warmth of two log fires (real logs and coal, not gas!) while in summer there is the pleasure of an enclosed garden. Since the pub holds a Children's Licence, families can enjoy a meal in the cosy dining room.

With the exception of Sunday evenings, meals are served lunchtimes and evenings from Tuesday onwards, with menus to suit most tastes. At lunchtime there is a choice of chicken and fish dishes, lasagnes and ploughman's, baguettes and sandwiches, with further choices from the daily blackboard menu. Substantial steak dishes are added to the evening menu, roast lunches to the Sunday menu. Sunday lunches are in great demand, so it is well worth booking a table in advance!

Good real ales are always available, also German and French wines; and to round off the meal, freshly ground coffee. And you may find yourself pleasurably entertained by the pub's quality pianola! Telephone: 01923 262261.

The Walk

① With your back to the Plough's front entrance, walk along Dunny Lane in the direction of Sarratt and Croxley Green. Leave the road where it divides (100 yards or so) and branch left into a drive – a no through road – signposted to Penman's

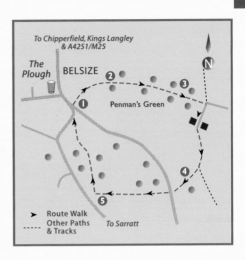

Green. Bungalows accompany the drive as it climbs steeply to the wooded heights of the Green.

② Ignore a footpath branching off to the left before you enter the wood and soon find yourself beside an information board outlining the history of Penman's Green. Woodruff and Heather Cottage are over the left from this point. As explained on the board, the long narrow Green was once an open grassy area where sheep were penned and watered on their way to market. With the profuse growth of trees and hedgerows now kept in check the green has become a haven for wildlife. Take the right-hand of two ways from this point (the other is for horses) and proceed through the wood not far from its right-hand border.

③ You will eventually pass a pond to your left, with an old cherry orchard nearby. The pond was once a watering hole for the penned-in sheep. Keeping forward from the pond go through a pedestrians' gap and soon turn right at a crossing. Passing

Some of the attractive cottages to be found in Belsize

Hillmeads Farm Cottage, follow the drive to the farm itself. Go through a gate on the left just beyond a stable and keep forward for 100 yards to a stile. Follow the field edge ahead until it curves left after 120 yards. Turn right here, crossing the field and passing an isolated oak tree. A waymark arrow points the way.

④ Soon follow a wood edge and descend the hill to a gate and stile; then keep forward across what was once a long narrow field to another stile and a lane. Turn right at the lane and, after only 40 yards, cross a stile on the left. Go uphill through this lovely wood, keeping within a few yards of its left-hand border. You will pass a number of deep pits to your right before arriving at another road – a road which you should ignore!

⑤ Staying in the wood turn right and walk the gently rising waymarked path to a stile. Leave the wood here and follow a left-hand field edge, with an excellent view of Belsize ahead – including its prominent red telephone box! When the field edge goes off to the left, turn right and cross the field downhill to a stile and a road – Poles Hill. Turning right at the road join Dunny Lane at the bottom and enjoy again the welcoming sight of the Plough.

PLACES OF INTEREST NEARBY

Chipperfield Common with its cricket green, ancient chestnut trees and Apostle's Pond, is less than a mile from Belsize. The approach is along Dunny Lane in the King's Langley direction followed by a second right turn into Windmill Hill.